D0709722

Deus caritas est.
God is love.

Contents

Editorial Note

This book is not a biography of Benedict XVI. It focuses only on his time in office as Pope. Immediately after his retirement, Professor Stefan Heid, the head historian of the Görres Society in Rome in the Campo Santo Teutonico beside Saint Peter's Basilica, asked me whether I would like to publish my articles about Benedict as a book, so that they would not be lost as documents of contemporary events. That was the basic impulse for this anthology. This book therefore begins precisely on April 18, 2005, at 5:45 p.m. and ends on February 28, 2013, at 6:00 p.m. with a final *"Buona notte"* [Good night] from the balcony of the Papal Palace in Castel Gandolfo. It covers eight years, or more precisely: 94 months, or 2,871 days, or 68,904 hours, and it consists of a selection of various essays in which I described Benedict XVI in that time as a correspondent for *Die Welt* in Rome and while traveling. The articles were abridged here and there, but nothing was added to them years later as prophetic foreknowledge. They were never "enriched" with later information.

Almost all the pieces were written under pressure, especially with the time constraints of a deadline, mostly under stress and often in adventurous conditions, while traveling, in media centers, outdoors, in hotel rooms, always beside a ringing telephone on which colleagues in Berlin were pressing for submission. The quantity of text, too, is almost always determined by the editor's specifications. The pieces include reportage, human interest stories, news, essays, and lead articles. Many articles are very personal reflections of that time in office. Nor does the collection cover the pontificate completely, because my colleagues by no means found interesting and important everything that seemed so in Rome, and also because a heart attack and a case of pneumonia interrupted my work in those years for two rather long periods. Often in those eight years, I see today, I was much weaker than the old Pope.

Then too, many journeys of the Pope were so long and so distant, for example to Sidney or Brazil, that the publisher found it too expensive to send a correspondent. During the triumphal trip through the U.S.A., on the other hand, when the Pope commemorated the victims of September 11, 2001, at the ruins of the Twin Towers on the eve of Passover 2008, I was in the hospital with a ticket for the flight. For health reasons I was out of commission for the entire year 2008, which is why I had to reconstruct somewhat the chapter for that time period today and fit it into this collection after the fact. Moreover this collection of articles is not free of contradictory evaluations. I deleted repetitions that are superfluous today. These are always snapshots, which nevertheless, reread one after the other, shed light on the drama of this pontificate in a way that surprised even me as I reviewed them—perhaps me most of all. In retrospect this anthology reads almost like the chronology of a failure heralded in advance. Yet it was not a failure. It was greatness.

Moreover this book offers in a certain way original historical sources. It is a fragment in which, as though in old shards of pottery, one can discern the chronicle of an almost superhuman struggle, and also his boldness and courage—and the almost overwhelming hostilities against which the Pope from Germany (and also precisely for that reason, as a German) saw himself pitted in those eight years from the beginning. The shy and so exceedingly kind man met with more ill will than any Pope in decades. More than a lot of analyses, the rereading of these observations made his resignation comprehensible—whereby my initial lack of understanding finally yielded to the question: How on earth did the old man put up with it for so long?

Like a piece of amber, though, this document also captures—without later interpretation—various steps for which Benedict XVI will go down in history: There is of course his resignation, like that of Emperor Charles V in the year 1555 or that of the Abruzzese Pope Celestine V in the year 1294. The rescue of the liturgy of all times for the Catholic Church. His genuflection—the first by a Pope in 476 years—before the Holy Veil of Manoppello on September 1, 2006, which he brought back into history with a silent prayer.

All his books, his struggle to reconcile faith and reason (and to purify both), and his giant steps toward Judaism will probably last—and the fact that he was the first postmodern man in the shoes of the fisherman. As one of his first official acts he abolished shortly after his election one of the originally nine traditional titles of the Pope: "Patriarch of the West." But until then he still was that nevertheless. For a short time he was the last Patriarch of the West. The concept of "the West," though, is understood today only by a minority. In history the so comprehensively educated Joseph Ratzinger will therefore probably go down as the last European on the Throne of Peter.

But perhaps one thing above all is true about this book: it originated from a very close-up view of Benedict XVI, who in those years was Pope in the first place, but secondly my neighbor too. And this also is true: I have missed him, since the light went out in his room over Saint Peter's Square on February 28, 2013. I love him very much.

Paul Badde, Rome, 2016

Benedict Up Close

Habemus papam:
Epochal Change in Rome — 2005

A great joy — Rome, April 19, 2005[1]
Relief is the first thing in the features of Pope Benedict XVI. He throws his arms high over Saint Peter's Square like a boxer. All the weight of the world that seems often to have oppressed and shackled Joseph Cardinal Ratzinger, as recently as yesterday, has suddenly fallen away from him. Once again he throws his arms high, and again! No one has ever seen him this way, not even he himself. Nothing is too big for him, not the crimson stole, not the white skullcap, not even the shoes of his predecessor, whose neighbor and closest confidant he was for over two decades. Even yesterday he climbed unnoticed with his secretary into a little Fiat Golf, but as of today he has moved house, to a place not a hundred meters away, just across the street. Yet it looks now as if he had taken an apartment in heaven, as if he could fly right away. He will never see his old apartment again. Indescribable rejoicing welcomes him on the Chair of Peter, first from the masses on

---

[1] The dateline of an article does not necessarily reflect the exact day or days described by the author in that article. — Ed.

3

Saint Peter's Square, then by the Romans, then by the Italians, and finally by the bewildered world, and even more by the Universal Church, which is suddenly being headed and led by one of the most brilliant and accomplished minds on the globe. That is truly an epochal change. One of the wisest minds in Europe on the most distinguished chair in the West, after generations of intellectuals have turned their backs on the Church.

A white wisp of smoke introduced this change, at 5:45 p.m., which was observed skeptically by millions of pairs of eyes. Was it white, or was it gray again after all? Won't the color change again? No, definitively, it was white. It's just that the sky is gray. And then it was already clear, too: Of all the cardinals, only Joseph Ratzinger can have won the election so swiftly, the first German in centuries in the shoes of the fisherman Simon from the Sea of Gennesaret. For a moment the telephone network broke down. Laughter and shouts from a thousand throats. Joy wafted like a storm over the thousand heads toward Saint Peter's Basilica. The bells started, slowly at first, cautiously, until they grew to a final frantic crescendo, for almost twenty minutes. Only now does all the hesitation and all the doubt dissolve completely into ultimate rejoicing. No soccer stadium has ever witnessed such frenzy.

It started even before the new Pope appeared before the crowd. A light rain set in, drop by drop, like tears. All the spotlights around the square started up, over the Bernini columns, over the houses in the vicinity, on the Gianicolo Hill, bright and glistening. Somewhere a rainbow must have formed right away over the square. In the colonnades a drum roll approached. The Swiss Guard marched in, wearing their most splendid uniforms. Behind them the bands of the *carabinieri* [police], of the Italian Army, of the Navy, and of the Air Force. Suddenly the curtains behind the glass door over the *Loggia* [balcony] were pulled back.

The red velvet fell down as Cardinal Estévez stepped forward and exclaimed: "*Annuntio vobis gaudium magnum; habemus Papam: Eminentissimum ac Reverendissimum Dominum, Dominum Josephum Sanctae Romanae Ecclesiae Cardinalem Ratzinger qui sibi nomen imposuit Benedictum XVI.* — I announce to you a great joy: we have a Pope: the Most Eminent and Most Reverend Lord Joseph Ratzinger, Cardinal of the Holy Roman Church, who has taken for himself the name Benedict XVI."

Only then did the new Pope himself step forward. "Dear Brothers and Sisters," he said before his first blessing, "After the great Pope John Paul II, the Cardinals have elected me, a simple and humble laborer in the vineyard of the Lord. The fact that the Lord knows how to work and to act even with inadequate instruments comforts me, and above all I entrust myself to your prayers. Let us move forward in the joy of the Risen Lord, confident of his unfailing help. The Lord will help us, and Mary, his Most Holy Mother, will be on our side. Thank you."

Farewell to the man in black — Rome, April 20, 2005

I will never see and experience Joseph Ratzinger again this way after yesterday evening: beside the monitor of my PC; through the Venetian blinds in front of my window; behind the rosemary that the wind now wafts through; the way he walks along in the evening dusk through the Via del Mascherino where it ends in the Via delle Grazie in order to stretch his legs. His steps had something of the regular beat of a metronome. Almost always he was alone. At the bookstore ahead and to the left he would stand in front of the display window, looking at the latest titles. Throughout his life, books were the great passion of this lonely pedestrian — and curiosity about ever-new titles. Every day newly published volumes, each with a different dedication, were placed on his desk, which already was groaning under tomes that one human being can scarcely manage. Nevertheless, he noted every single title, even though during one of our last meetings in the colonnades he sighed, "How am I supposed to be able to read all that?" Yet he tried again and again, he could not do otherwise. A frail old man in black, wrapped up in his simple coat against the wintry cold, his shoulders more and more stooped in recent years, with a Basque beret like a village priest, and beneath it the hair that for years has been so snow white that yesterday evening you had to look twice at the *Loggia* to tell that this time the white skullcap of the popes was on his head.

It is just about two hundred steps from our house to the old front door of his residence on the Piazza della Città Leonina—which he left forever on Sunday morning before the Conclave; from now on he will spend his life on the other side of the street, behind Saint Anne's Gate, on the top floor of the Apostolic Palace. Maybe he will find more peace and quiet there. Hopefully he is now somewhat better protected there. We can expect this protection from the Swiss Guard rather than from the policemen at his front door. During world crises there were often two automobiles in which the officers smoked with the windows open and watched soccer games on little televisions. So it was back then. I never saw bodyguards at his side. Even last Saturday only his secretary held for him the door of a little Ford in front of his house, in which the two men then rounded the corner like a dean with his assistant priest.

Anyone who got up early enough could meet him every morning, as he hurried with his briefcase diagonally across Saint Peter's Square to his desk in the Holy Office. Every Thursday in the early morning he used to celebrate Holy Mass in German in the Campo Santo Teutonico. Cardinal Ratzinger's security was never entirely of this world, nor was the authority of this former successor to the Grand Inquisitors. His security consisted most often in the shyness with which he hurried through the streets of the Borgo like a deer, with bright, alert eyes that nothing seemed to escape. He always used to see and recognize me even from a distance. For years now I have encountered him often. Many years ago, at a reception at the *Bayerischer Hof* in Munich, I once poured a glass of champagne on my suit as he made his way toward me through the crowd: "Herr Badde!"

That was when he presented *Salt of the Earth*: a book-length interview that he had granted to my friend Peter Seewald. I don't know how many letters and greetings he received from me — and I from him. In a certain way we could not get away from each other — not even with my apartment, which was finally offered to me right there in his neighborhood, after I had received from him shortly before a long letter in Jerusalem. *"Divina provvidenza"* he would call that, "Divine Providence," as he always did when he seemed to lapse into Italian, when he wanted to use words that seemed to have lost their value in German like an old, devalued currency.

On one spring evening not long ago we walked again together over Saint Peter's Square; after Christmas I met him once again in the middle of the crowd, through which he made his way as unnoticed as though he were wearing a cloak of invisibility. But now I remember most of all a sunny late afternoon last September, when I met him just as I was bringing two full trash bags to the trash bins down in the Via del Mascherino. "Herr Badde!" he said again in his high-pitched voice. He grinned at me in embarrassment and held out his hand toward me, while I still had my hands full. It was a bit awkward. He wanted to thank me cordially for an article in *Die Welt* about a miraculous image of the Face of Christ on a cloth, he said, that I had discovered in the Abruzzi region. It is the Face of the Risen Christ, the origin of which is utterly mysterious. The material of this transparent photograph consists of byssus: sea silk. Yet the fabric cannot be painted at all.

The topic fascinated Joseph Ratzinger, whom nothing enthralls so much as the marvelous Incarnation of the Son of God, whom he serves as Vicar since yesterday. After that meeting I sent him my last letter. From the last sea silk weaver in the Mediterranean I had received a bundle of that puzzling silk derived from mussels. Even this yarn was a little treasure: the gold of the sea, softer than cashmere wool, finer than angel's hair. In the sun it gleams like copper. I put this tuft in an envelope and asked Cardinal Ratzinger whether he could hold it up in the sun in front of the eyes of the ailing Holy Father, who after all had spent his entire life seeking the Face of God. Whether that ever happened, I do not know. But on Monday I had to think of it again as Cardinal Ratzinger said in his homily before the beginning of the Conclave that Christ has revealed to us "His Face, His Heart." Behind the little man beneath the baldachin in the middle of Saint Peter's Basilica a gigantic marble figure held over his head a veil with the image of Christ on it. I do not know whether Joseph Ratzinger was able to forward my last present to John Paul II. But since he became Benedict XVI yesterday, my bundle of sea silk has finally ended up in the hands of the Holy Father after all.

Change of pilot on a sinking boat — Rome, April 21, 2005

It was often said about Joseph Ratzinger that he would sooner have to be "carried to the hunt" than be driven by ambition into the wilderness of business or academia in pursuit of big game. In a Jewish *shtetl* in Eastern Poland before the war they probably would have called him an "airhead" [*Luftmensch*]: a bookworm staring into space who often seemed to hover over the ground of reality rather than to walk on it. The question of how this man from Marktl am Inn, a village in Bavaria, managed to have such a steep career path in the world's largest global enterprise therefore transcends even the miraculous element also that has often been talked about these days. He was always called; he never pushed himself forward. At the conclusion he was called no longer by a college of professors but by God himself, as Cardinals Wetter and Meisner both said on Tuesday evening in Rome about this step; otherwise this election cannot be understood at all.

Joseph Ratzinger was never a careerist. The careerists were many of the others who did not have this career. This went on well into the Conclave, where some of the cardinals urgently tried once again to thwart his election. "Pay no attention to your careers," Pope John Paul II had urged the cardinals at the last Consistory that he had called in Autumn of 2003. The crimson of their robes, after all, reminds them of the blood that they should be ready to shed for the Church if necessary. Consequently there can and must be no thought about a career. Nevertheless, the Pope had to pronounce this admonition to the Senate of the Catholic Church publicly on Saint Peter's Square.

This warning cannot have been and probably was not meant for Joseph Ratzinger. Rather, he would have had this man in mind as an example for the others. For this man, his most trusted adviser, strikingly lacked the ability and the temperament required for intrigue. This had often been construed as a sign of his weak leadership ability, and they will probably keep saying that in the future too as he exercises the most important leadership office in the largest Church in the world. Joseph Ratzinger himself, however, recently spelled out once again how in the paradox of the Church every career ladder that really leads upward should be understood: It must be a ladder that leads up to the Cross.

On March 25, less than a month ago, he replaced the deathly ill Pope on Good Friday in front of the Colosseum during the traditional Way of the Cross. Moreover he himself had written the meditations and prayers for it. "Should we not also think of how much Christ suffers in His own Church?" he sighed in his meditation on the Ninth Station, where Jesus collapses for the third time under the weight of the Cross. "How often is his Word twisted and misused! What little faith is present behind so many theories, so many empty words! How much filth there is in the Church, and even among those who, in the priesthood, ought to belong entirely to him! How much pride, how much self-complacency! ... Lord, your Church often seems like a boat about to sink, a boat taking in water on every side. In your field we see more weeds than wheat. The soiled garments and face of your Church throw us into confusion. Yet it is we ourselves who have soiled them! It is we who betray you time and time again, after all our lofty words and grand gestures."

And now Joseph Ratzinger himself stands on the bridge of this boat as the new pilot who in the evening dusk of Good Friday continued with the words: "Let us halt ... before the suffering Son of God.... Let us try to see His Face in the people we might look down upon.... Let us nail ourselves to Him, resisting the temptation to stand apart, or to join others in mocking Him.... Amid the decay of ideologies, our faith needs once more to be the fragrance which returns us to the path of life."

Passover on Saint Peter's Square—Rome, April 24, 2005

Pesach has begun, the Jewish feast of the "Passover of the Lord." Therefore no honorary guests can come from Jerusalem to the Vatican for the enthronement of the newly elected monarch of Christendom. The Passover rest does not allow it. The chief rabbis of Rome, nevertheless, hurried together to Saint Peter's Square, where this Sunday the final tableau of a divine transition will be completed, such as the people of the media age have not yet seen. From the death of John Paul II to the installation of Benedict XVI, Saint Peter's Square has become the stage of a breathtaking world theater. The obelisk in the middle—a cosmic antenna. For weeks now it has been broadcasting from here into the world images from a picture gallery that it will take a long time to interpret. High above in the Apostolic Palace the shutters have been drawn in front of the Pope's windows. He has not yet moved in.

The coat of arms on the claret-colored velvet curtain in front of the *Loggia* of the Basilica is still empty. We can still speculate about what he will say there about his program. Yet the transition is now completed. Benedict XVI has taken the silver shepherd's staff of John Paul II like the baton in a relay race. At the beginning the big screens on Saint Peter's Square show how in the crypt of the Basilica before the tomb of the Apostle Peter he lingers in silent prayer, in a gold robe, with his ringless hand placed on his breast as though for protection. Then he walks behind the cardinals into the mild light of this Roman spring day as though into a new century.

Whereas on April 8 he still wore a crimson robe as he incensed the coffin of his great predecessor with a censer, now he walks around the altar with the same censer and from there goes to the cross, this time in this faintly glimmering, billowing gold robe, before finally sitting down then on the throne, where for such a painfully long time a wheelchair had to be pushed for his predecessor. Kings and potentates, enthralled, watch every gesture of the graceful man from left and right, as do the eyes of millions of Romans and pilgrims on the square and in the city. Flags wave over the sea of the crowd, today with a little more of the black-red-and-gold of the German flag, although basically it has remained the same combination of colors of the United Nations that meet here again and again.

The flowers decorating Saint Peter's Square are sparser than at Easter, when usually whole truckloads are sent to Rome from Holland. The flame of the Easter candle behind the altar shivers in its globe that protects it from the wind. Normalcy seems here to stay, as the new Bishop of Rome prepares to celebrate the Eucharist with the Church for the first time, in a "feast of faith," as he says. Yet there is no peaceful normalcy in matters of faith. Even the first reading from the Acts of the Apostles says in a few words the very same thing as the document *Dominus Iesus* (Jesus the Lord), for which Joseph Cardinal Ratzinger reaped a whirlwind of indignation years ago. Jesus "is the stone which was rejected by you builders, but which has become the cornerstone. And there is salvation in no one else, for there is no other name under heaven given among men by which we must be saved." That is the message of this feast of faith.

One and all, these are readings during which you hold your breath, since honorary guests from all cultures are here, silently putting up with them between the Gregorian chants. The Gospel is sung in Latin and Greek—out of the two lungs of Europe that the last Pope always spoke about—yet one of the voices today seems deeper and more powerful than the other as it rolls back and forth between Bernini's marble columns. Hearts pound in the crowd lower down, to which Benedict XVI in a high-pitched voice presents an ancient Greek greeting of peace. He will not expound any program for his reign, he says in his homily, and then he quickly moves on to speak about the unabridged message of the Church that he intends to proclaim.

This can and must be expected of this new Pope, therefore: He will not delete one line of *Dominus Iesus*, whom he as the Chief Shepherd of the Church will of course present anew again and again to all fellow Christians, but also to the Jews, as well as to "all our contemporaries, believers and unbelievers." He shines with self-confidence, he smiles with new composure. In the death of Pope John Paul II, it became clear to the whole world, he exclaims, that the ancient "Church is alive and young." For "Christ lives and is risen." It is a homily about the next world, with which he will shake this world as well like an earthquake. For today he definitively joins forces with John Paul II, the great man above him "at the window of the Father's house," with whom he shared countless hours here below. Together with him he now explains the signs that he allows the bishops to place on him here: the "pallium" of the good shepherd who brings the lost sheep back home on his shoulders, and the "fisher ring" of the fisher of men. "Out of the desert!" he now shouts to the world together with his predecessor. "To the waters of life," where everyone again becomes aware that he is not "some casual and meaningless product of evolution ... [but] the result of a thought of God." "Each of us is necessary."

It is a speech in which at the conclusion he once again bows deeply before his predecessor—and before his inaugural speech on October 22, 1978: "Do not be afraid to welcome Christ and accept His power.... Do not be afraid. Open wide the doors for Christ. To His saving power open the boundaries of States, economic and political systems, the vast fields of culture, civilization and development. Do not be afraid." Benedict XVI knows of course about the other boundaries and walls that have grown since then. Yet no one has ever seen him as fearless, free, and courageous as today. The speech is wonderful. Only his courage is no surprise. Now he has entered a complete unity with John Paul II. In these days the Church will be ruled by two popes—from heaven and from earth.

The Incarnation and becoming human — Rome, June 13, 2005

On Sunday afternoon several thousand more people appeared again beneath the window of Pope Benedict XVI to pray the Angelus together than on the previous Sunday. This time even the quadrilateral Piazza Pio XII in front of the elliptical oval of Saint Peter's Square was filled. That had never happened in recent years even during the reign of John Paul II. Since his election in April the German Pope magnetically draws more people to Rome from week to week. But those who had expected him to take once again at this prominent place a stance concerning the referendum in which Italy's voters were to vote on Sunday and Monday about four different articles of a new law on bioethics found themselves disappointed. Instead, Benedict XVI called for regular attendance at the celebration of the Eucharist, because Christians "cannot live without Sunday." Afterward he recited the Angelus in Latin as usual.

Nevertheless, many Italians probably still understand that the reminder that the Pope thereby proclaims to the world week after week leaves the Church no other alternative, basically, than to defend every human life uncompromisingly from the moment of conception. For "the angel of the Lord" reminds us, after all, of the moment of Christ's "Incarnation," exactly nine months before His birth. So it can hardly be otherwise: Catholics think that every other human being too should enjoy all human rights from the moment of his or her conception: first and foremost the right to life. Logically therefore they cannot approve of a human embryo being understood and treated merely as "vegetative tissue."

Shalom aleikhem — Cologne, August 19, 2005

Knee deep like Hindus in the Ganges, the pilgrims stood in the Rhine on Thursday in Cologne and perched enraptured in the trees alongside the streets. He encountered "an explosion of joy," Benedict XVI says early Friday morning. Today the Pope from Germany will visit for the first time, shortly before the beginning of the Sabbath, the oldest synagogue on German soil. The whole world will watch him. "Benedict had his opportunity," a colleague from an international news agency says knowingly in the early morning after a first glance at the outline of the speech that the Pope will give at the synagogue in Cologne at noon, "and he did not take it! He is a German, after all. He should speak louder here!" But even after his election, Benedict XVI is a man who speaks softly. Nevertheless, in the manuscript for the speech horrible noises reecho: the wailing of women and children who had to pack their things when they were expelled from Cologne in 1424. The rumbling of the freight cars. The cries from the depths of Auschwitz. It is a story of sighing and mourning, in the presence of which, in the words of John Paul II, he "bow[s] [his] head before all who experienced this manifestation of the *mysterium iniquitatis*." But before he recalls this "mystery of evil," Abraham Lehrer, the leader of the community in Cologne offered in Aramaic in the memorial room of the synagogue a mourner's "kaddish," the prayer for the dead said by sons for their fathers, which this morning, however, recalls the more than 11,000 Jews of Cologne who were murdered and the six million Jews of Europe who were swept into the abyss by Hitler's murderous machine. Lehrer's mother sits in the audience; she still has on her arm the number that the Nazis branded her with. That is the miracle of this day: the fact that sixty years after that crime she now sits in the synagogue in Cologne in order to greet the Pope from Germany.

You hardly dare to turn your head around to all the bishops and honorary guests, all with a similar skullcap: the *kippah* or *yarmulke* of the Jews and the *pileolus* or *zucchetto* of the Catholics. The strange similarity is perplexing. The large Romanesque rose window, the liturgical vestments, the tabernacle for the Torah scrolls, the seven-branched candelabra, the prayer shawls of the leaders of the congregation—or the shofar, the ram's horn of the shepherds from the wilderness of Judea, which is sounded here in Cologne on the Rhine. To Catholic eyes everything is as close as it is strange—as strange and as close as Psalm 23, which the cantor Chaim Adler sings in Hebrew: "I fear no evil; for you are with me, Lord."

The Pope at the podium, serious and concentrating deeply, is probably one of the few people in the room who understand it without translation. After all the introductory speakers, he begins his speech with a quiet "*Shalom aleikhem*"—the ancient greeting of peace with which Jesus greeted his apostles: "Peace be with you!" After that he enters into the remembrance that Natanael Teitelbaum began before him—yet it is like a song that is sung to two different melodies. They are variations on

a theme that mutually enrich and expand each other. Teitelbaum acknowledges the "seven commandments of the sons of
Noah" which God gave the world as a natural law: as the civi-
lizational minimum of all human culture, as the foundation of
any dialogue. The Pope, in contrast, sees precisely in the Jewish
"Decalogue" of Moses, in the Ten Commandments, our "shared
legacy and commitment. The Ten Commandments are not a
burden, but a signpost showing the path leading to a successful life." The Patriarch Abraham is for Jews and Christians the
"father in faith." Therefore it is also true that "Whoever meets
Jesus Christ meets Judaism."

Teitelbaum recalls among his "five Jewish pillars for peace" in
particular remembrance as the second pillar—even Napoleon
in Akko acknowledged that a people like the Jewish people,
which 2,000 years after the destruction of the Temple was still
lamenting that misfortune, "will without fail have a future too."
A few minutes later the Pope puts his finger on the fact that the
long, tense history of Jews and Christians took a mad turn into
murderous catastrophe when too many Europeans tried to get rid
of their Christian faith—so as to exchange it for a "neo-pagan
racist ideology." "The holiness of God was no longer recognized,
and consequently, contempt was shown for the sacredness of
human life." Therefore the remembrance of this terrible development must henceforth "never cease to rouse consciences, to
resolve conflicts, to inspire the building of peace"—in "great
esteem for Muslims" as well.

It is as if an endlessly deep sigh in the history between Jews
and Christians were emerging in all the speeches, yet today it is
also as if they were leaning on one another in exhaustion. "Cologne embraces the Pope," the Italian press reported on Friday in
astonishment; yet in this hour it is also as if the Christian Church

'and Judaism were embracing, the "*Ecclesia*" and the "Synagogue," once again as allegorically and cordially as in an ancient mosaic—nevertheless, after all the quarreling and failure almost at the end now and not right at the beginning of a centuries-old history of salvation and calamity. The big rabbi extends to the little Pope his mighty hand at the end of his speech. The Pontifex Maximus, in contrast, the "supreme bridge builder," ends his speech with words from Psalm 29: "May the LORD give strength to his people! May the LORD bless his people with peace!" According to the Catholic persuasion, however, this "people" comprises both Jews and Christians. That is not a dream. It is a promise. In Cologne, however, it seems today for a few moments to be reality.

The power of transformation—Cologne, August 21, 2005

During the Sign of Peace that the Pope exchanged with his friend Cardinal Meisner during the celebration of the Eucharist on Sunday, millions around the world could tell that he is not yet comfortable with all too much closeness. He is a master of the fingertips. Robust embraces seem foreign to him. For the new Pontifex Maximus, crowds are dreadful from the word go. "For Benedict XVI, World Youth Day in Cologne is an ordeal," the journalist Vittorio Messori wisely noted in Italy in an interview before the Pope's trip to Cologne. "World Youth Day is an initiative of Karol Wojtyła. Joseph Ratzinger would never have planned such an event. If he could have, he probably would have skipped it. He is in Cologne out of a sense of duty. As sure as I am acquainted with him, he is suffering. Masses of people and choirs in a stadium are not for him." It is true, and you can read it, too, on the Pope's face like a book: At least the many pop interludes during the liturgies are not to the taste of the pianist.

The subtle theologian is an aficionado of Gregorian chant and the old Latin liturgy. Unlike his predecessor, he was never an actor, mime, and singer. "John Paul II was a priest who participated in camping trips in the mountains," Messori notes. "His successor has lived his life in the subdued light of libraries. That is also why that duo functioned so well. John Paul II was extroverted, with a love for the theater, and charismatic. Joseph Ratzinger is pensive, aristocratic, with a keen intellect. He simply cannot find the right tone for ecclesiastical Woodstock festivals. The faith of John Paul II was instinctive and mystical. Ratzinger is a postmodern intellectual who believes despite his doubts. He proves with arguments that God exists and Jesus is His Son."

This is true—and it is almost as if even his handwriting reflected a little of the shy character of Benedict XVI. It is florid, old-fashioned, and so small that his own name in a little note that he wrote for the back side of a commemorative photograph had to be specially enlarged a bit. It is the motto of World Youth Day written with a fine-tipped fountain pen in Joseph Ratzinger's handwriting: "We have come to worship him (Matt. 2:2)—Benedict XVI—World Youth Day XX—Cologne, August 18-21, 2005." Monsignor Gänswein, his private secretary, pressed the memento into my hand late on Thursday evening, when I met him in the cathedral in Cologne, as relaxed as though he were just another pilgrim who was spending a day along the Rhine this rainy night. He fished the picture of the welcoming Pope out of his pocket and pressed it into my hand laughing, before being submerged again in the crowd of pilgrims and disappearing into the depths of this dark, sacred space toward the gold, glimmering shrine of the Three Kings in the raised choir of the cathedral.

Surely Benedict XVI would gladly have accompanied his secretary again unrecognized at this hour. But that is probably the one thing that he must deny himself and has denied himself during these days. The pilgrims would have crushed him—out of love and respect. Therefore everything that could be said about Benedict XVI before this World Youth Day is no longer true—or at most only half-true. He is no longer the same as he was before. In Cologne he received once again a final lesson in the school of John Paul II, and as always he brilliantly achieved the purpose of the class. He had learned by now in Rome to wade in the crowd. As of Cologne, he now knows also how to swim in the sea of the masses. Forty years after Woodstock he hits here the high C of the young people like no other pop star. "I know that you as young people have great aspirations," he calls to the young people before they journey home, to uproarious rejoicing. "Let others see this, let the world see it . . . , and through your love above all, the world will be able to discover the star that we follow as believers."

It is as though John Paul II had transformed the university professor into an elementary school student again in this examination in Cologne. Christ "instructed us to enter into his 'hour,'" he explains to the immense multitude of his pupils on the nature of the Eucharist. "We enter into it through the sacred power of the words of consecration." It is a transformation of the sort that is evident in the saints: "In their lives, as if in a great picture-book, the riches of the Gospel are revealed. They are the shining path which God Himself has traced throughout history and is still tracing today." They are the real achievers of renewal, the true reformers. "Now I want to express this in an even more radical way: only from the saints, only from God does true revolution come, the definitive way to change the world."

Suddenly the evening sky opens over Marienfeld. The previous day it rained and poured, today for hours on end it was menacingly gray, now the cosmos gleams as clear as a shimmering paten over Marienfeld, in a circle cut out of the gray, dense sea of clouds that hangs in the heights over all of Germany. Only one single high-flying cloud towers as a changing shape beside the sky over the altar, with streaks of cirrus clouds above it, as though they were the tails of many stars and comets.

"Absolutizing what is not absolute but relative is called totalitarianism," the Pope continues in his history lesson, and then he warmly recommends "two thoughts" to his gigantic class: "There are many who speak of God; some even preach hatred and perpetrate violence in God's Name. So it is important to discover the true Face of God. The Magi from the East found it when they knelt down before the Child of Bethlehem.... In Jesus Christ, who allowed His heart to be pierced for us, the true Face of God is seen. We will follow Him together with the great multitude of those who went before us. Then we will be travelling along the right path." Then to this basic course given on the artificial hill built out of earth brought from all over the world to the gates of Cologne, he adds another papal lesson on physics, about "nuclear fission in the very heart of being"—in the victory of love over hatred, in the victory of love over death, in an "intimate explosion of good conquering evil." Only this explosion "can trigger off the series of transformations that little by little will change the world." It is a matter of making God's word about the beginning of creation ("It is good") come true over and over again and to prove it right. There is no more appropriate way of doing this than adoration, which the Three Wise Men from the East too had set out to do. But adoration in Latin means "*ad-oratio*": "mouth-to-mouth contact, a kiss, an embrace, and hence, ultimately love." Joseph Ratzinger is saying that, the new Pope to whom robust embraces are still foreign. Thus World Youth Day transformed the city of Cologne and Marienfeld—and Benedict XVI.

Benedict Up Close

Homosexuals in the Church and in
the Vatican—Rome, November 23, 2005

The Vatican has many leaks. Out of one of these places that are
not watertight a strong, two-and-a-half-page Italian document
on "Criteria for the Discernment of Vocations to the Priesthood
in Persons with Homosexual Tendencies" has now reached the
public after being polished for years, even though it was supposed to remain strictly confidential until it was officially published in late November. There is nothing surprising or exciting
about that. First, it is nothing new that the obligatory celibacy
of Catholic priests has always made this state in life especially
attractive to male homosexuals also. Realistically, nobody can
deny that the Catholic Church has therefore had significantly
greater experience precisely with homosexuals.

The leaks in the many halls of the Vatican are not surprising,
nor is the fact that there are quite a few gays in clerical garb (in
those same halls too), nor the new attitude in the guidelines that
the Vatican has now issued on this topic. Or maybe they are after
all. For many Catholics had hoped that the new Pope would take
a strong stance against men with homosexual inclinations in the
ranks of the priesthood. Especially in the United States, where
a flood of homosexual affairs [sic] with children or adolescents
within the Church has driven whole dioceses into ruin in recent
years, or else in Austria, where a homosexual subculture led last
year to papal orders to close the major seminary in Sankt Pölten.

But such a condemnation was not forthcoming. Specifically
the document does not deal at all with gays who have been
priests for a long time now, but rather with "the admission or
non-admission to Holy Orders of (new) candidates" with homosexual inclinations. As far as homosexual "acts" are concerned,

the document does not deviate from the *Catechism*'s terms of reference, in which a long tradition of condemnation in this matter is summarized in the following words: such acts are "disordered."

Now candidates with "homosexual" inclinations, in contrast, are not generally and categorically excluded from the priesthood. Benedict XVI only demands once again strict chastity from them—and that they have provided proof of having practiced continence in this way for at least three years before their ordination to the priesthood. That is perhaps the most blatant weakness of the document. For in the broad and highly complex field of sexuality, no more than chastity is demanded of heterosexual priests in the Catholic Church, after all; in no instance must they provide proof of it for at least three years "before ordination." Besides, this very "proof" could be produced in either case only with the greatest difficulty. "It would be gravely dishonest for a candidate to hide his own homosexuality in order to proceed, despite everything, towards [priestly] ordination," the conclusion of the document says rather lamely. A second weakness in it, moreover, is the distinction between "homosexual tendencies" and "deep-seated homosexual tendencies." According to the terms of the document, those from the second group (in contrast to those from the first) "who practice homosexuality, present deep-seated homosexual tendencies, or support the so-called 'gay culture'" can no longer be admitted to Holy Orders in the future.

This could have been described much more simply and plausibly in the nineteenth century, because the gays meant here are obviously those who do not intend to practice the rather chivalrous virtue of chastity at all, even as priests. In the same situation, would anyone object if the Vatican were to apply the document to heterosexual candidates for the priesthood as well?

That is rather unlikely — even though it would be perhaps more understandable if such a document were to read, for instance, that candidates (regardless of their inclinations) "who freely engage in sexual relations, indulge their unrestrained libido, and are public supporters of a hedonistic culture" will no longer be admitted "to Holy Orders" in the future. In any case the Vatican will not be able to count on forbearance from the prevailing culture of the West with regard to this extremely explosive topic. Therefore in the next few days everyone is sure to forget the express admonition that all persons who must be barred from admission to the ordained priesthood of the Catholic Church deserve to be treated "with respect and sensitivity," whereby "every sign of unjust discrimination in their regard is to be avoided." Forgotten too will be the reminder that according to Church teaching there is no such thing as "a right to receive sacred ordination." The only point that will be highlighted anew, then, is the fact that the celibate — chaste and unmarried — priesthood is and remains a stumbling block in itself.

From Auschwitz via Regensburg to Turkey: The Minefield of Words — 2006

Love promises eternity — Rome, January 25, 2006

Love is not always the same love. There is filial love, puppy love, love of neighbor, love of money, love of God. Yet "love between man and woman, where body and soul are inseparably joined and human beings glimpse an apparently irresistible promise of happiness," Benedict XVI writes at the beginning of his first Encyclical, is nevertheless "the very epitome of love; all other kinds of love immediately seem to fade in comparison."

Encyclicals are papal teaching documents that express views about contemporary issues in a binding way. There are records of these ecclesiastical circular letters since the fourth century; as of the reign of Benedict XIV (1740-1758) they developed completely into an instrument in the governance of the Church. John Paul II during his long years in office composed fourteen such magisterial letters. Consequently people today have been waiting with great anticipation for the first programmatic statement of the new German Pope, which was published on Wednesday in Rome. A hundred years after Nietzsche he allows himself to be challenged once again by the philosopher's accusation that

Christianity poisoned *eros*. The "Nietzsche of the twentieth century," as Botho Strauss called the man on the papal throne, has now replied with a wealth of anecdotes and a mighty steeplechase through history and intellectual history.

The thing that fought the "perversion of religion," "healed" *eros*, and restored its true grandeur was not the "sacred" prostitution of antiquity, not the "divine madness" of paganism, not "simply submitting to instinct," but rather the biblical culture of the Old and New Testament, in which *eros* "tends to rise 'in ecstasy'" above the merely biological sphere "toward the Divine, to lead us beyond ourselves." The false divinization of *eros* has always in fact dehumanized it instead. For in contrast to all the other notions of divinity and fertility cults outside of the Bible, the God of the Bible loves man. The love for God of the Jews and the Christians is therefore always a response to—or a rejection of—this heavenly courtship. God loves first. The prophets Hosea and Ezekiel had already described His "passion for his people using boldly erotic images." This love "no longer is ... self-seeking, a sinking in the intoxication of happiness; instead it seeks the good of the beloved: it becomes renunciation and it is ready, and even willing, for sacrifice."

Moreover "this close connection between *eros* and marriage in the Bible (therefore) has practically no equivalent in extra-biblical literature." What is new in the biblical faith is evident therefore in "the image of God and the resulting image of mankind." "The real novelty of the New Testament lies not so much in new ideas as in the figure of Christ Himself, who gives flesh and blood to those concepts—an unprecedented realism." "Love promises eternity," Benedict XVI later replies almost tranquilly to the melancholy, useless sighing of Nietzsche's Zarathustra, which so obviously can never find fulfillment: "All pleasure wants eternity—wants deep, profound eternity!"

After the "purification of memory" that the Polish Pope had applied himself to in many of his writings, now the German Pope seems to pledge himself to a "purification of reason" and a "purification of love." In his case this becomes a moment of recollection in a new navigational position-finding of ecclesiastical identity. It is of course a reach for the stars. After the spectacular first part of his Encyclical, in which he traces a new picture of love (which "God is") as the center of Christian faith and the ground of Christian life and death, he devotes himself in the second part to a sort of rehabilitation of the charitable services of the Church, which he thereby brings back from the periphery into the center. He sees this *"caritas"* anew as the necessary growth of the Church beyond Herself with respect to the needs of the world; this had so astonished and fascinated Emperor Julian the Apostate, a declared opponent of the Christians in the fourth century, that he tried (in vain) to institute care for the needy in his design for a competitive pagan church. For *caritas* is the outward expression of the ecclesial "communion of love" into the world. This charity "will always prove necessary, even in the most just society," the Pope states categorically. But that is a final repudiation of the "vanished illusion" not just of Marxism, but also—and even more—of all totalitarian and integralist attempts and models within the Church and of Her theologians, who even a hundred years after Marx would still like to denounce all charitable initiatives as "serving that unjust system." This "is really an inhuman philosophy." The program of Christians must, in contrast, remain until the end of days "a heart which sees." Far beyond the current scene, Benedict XVI has presented with this first Encyclical an aid to those aid workers to whom the Church owes more glory than to all Her gothic and baroque basilicas. He himself simply calls the document "an invitation."

The Last Patriarch — Rome, March 3, 2006

Pope Benedict does not want to be a "Patriarch of the West" any more. This makes a little excursion through history necessary, perhaps first back to the year 380. At that time Emperor Theodosius I made the Nicene Creed of the Christians the mandatory faith of all subjects of Rome. It was a remarkable miracle. Only eighty years after the bloodiest persecution of Christians, the Catholic Church had suddenly become the obligatory state religion of the Roman Empire. Twelve years later the same Emperor prohibited all pagan worship; one year later he set fire to the Temple of Zeus in Olympia. Two years later he once again united the entire Roman Empire, although it broke up definitively into two parts after his death in the year 395 along with [sic] the newly liberated Church. [*The Church divided 650 years later.*] Located at that time in the Eastern Roman Empire, on whose territory Christianity had originated, were the venerable episcopal sees of Antioch, Alexandria, Jerusalem and Byzantium/Constantinople.

So far this little excursus should suffice to explain why Emperor Theodosius II, a grandson of Theodosius I, granted to the Roman bishop in the Western Roman Empire also the title of Patriarch. It was therefore the Emperor, not a Pope, who first made this claim. Since then, at any rate, the Successor of Peter was considered the "Patriarch of the West" along with the Patriarchs in the East. And after more than 1,500 years, Benedict XVI suddenly had this same title struck from the previous list of nine titles, without replacing it. There had been similar efforts already in the Middle Ages, when the popes of Rome no longer wanted to be considered on a par with the Eastern Patriarchs. The title, after all, never had a theological foundation either.

That, however, can only be an indication that the German Pope is adding the abolition of the title to the series of subtle signals with which he has previously stamped his first year in office. It is the claim of a new self-assurance as well as the abandonment of an old, unnecessary rivalry. Renouncing the title aims "to give expression to a historical and theological realism," the Vatican says. Giving up this claim is "a renunciation that could be useful and helpful to the ecumenical dialogue." Above all, however, the abandonment of this title is also the renunciation of an old restriction. The West is no longer enough for Benedict XVI.

The German hour in the Universal Church—Rome, May 8, 2006

Joseph Ratzinger was born on April 16, 1927, a Holy Saturday, in Marktl am Inn and was baptized a few hours later with the freshly blessed water from the Easter Vigil. The connection made a deep impression on him. Maybe he was already wide awake back then. Tomorrow, on his seventy-ninth birthday, the son of a policeman will give his Easter blessing for the first time to a billion Catholics and to the whole world in general (after the city of Rome). Via satellite his words will be broadcast to over sixty-five countries. No German has ever reached more people: Tomorrow Joseph Ratzinger celebrates his first Easter Sunday as Pope. It is a fitting occasion for a little German lesson.

In the beginning Germany was a Roman project. The land from which Germany emerged was for a long time called simply the "Roman Empire." In the floor of Saint Peter's Basilica there is still a remarkable trace of this: a circular slab of porphyry, ox-blood red, cracked in many places, right on the axis behind the main portal, behind and beneath the *Loggia* on which Joseph Ratzinger appeared in the public spotlight as Pope Benedict XVI for the first time one year ago. Ever since Saint Peter's Basilica was completed, the popes turn at this slab every time they leave their palace to go to a High Mass in the Basilica, making a right-angle turn to the right, toward the West, in order to walk to the main altar. Therefore you might also take the stone for a simple path marker. In fact it is a path marker of history.

The slab had already been embedded in the floor of the previous Basilica of Emperor Constantine. It was already there on Christmas Eve in the year 800 when Pope Leo III placed the imperial crown of the Roman Empire on the head of the Frankish King Charles of Aachen right on that same spot, even though there was another Roman Emperor at that time, albeit in the East. In the West, however, there was no longer a Roman Empire, since Western Rome had fallen in 476 during the Barbarian Invasions. With the chess move of crowning Charlemagne Emperor, Leo III caused this Roman Empire of the Franks to rise again abruptly in Rome at that time and even to travel over the Alps in a marvelous *"translatio."* This step had immense consequences. For Europe it was the great annexation of the North and the West to Rome's Church as well as to the Latin culture of the Mediterranean. The imperial foundation was to continue in existence through many vicissitudes for a good thousand years, although at first, from 800 until 1157 A.D., it remained merely the "Roman Empire."

Rainald of Dassel, the Chancellor of Emperor Barbarossa —and as Archbishop of Cologne a predecessor of Cardinal Meisner—was then the first to add to the Roman origin the aura of the "Holy" as well. (Shortly before that the relics of the Three Kings from the East had come to the Rhineland to *"hillije*

Kölle," Holy Cologne.) But then too, at the time when the "*Imperium Romanum*" was designated the "Holy Roman Empire," there would be no mention of "the Germans" or of their nation in documents for around four more centuries, until the genitive phrase "of the German Nation" was finally appended officially to the "Holy Roman Empire." It was the time when the nation state became more modern everywhere in Europe. The late reflection on the "German Nation" of its Empire is so to speak an early indication of the often even scurrilous emancipation process of the Germans, who until then had been attuned especially to regional and universal concerns, setting them on the narrower path of nationalism. In a certain way it was also, back then already, a sort of inferiority complex that they tried to cope with by this renaming in agreement with the strong new national states: of the Swedes and the Spaniards as well as of the French, the English, and the Swiss. About Arminius too ("Hermann" of the Cherusci tribe), to whom the Germans tried to trace themselves back as a sort of mythical ancestor many times later on when they had lost their way, they had learned for the first time (around 1,500 years after the Battle of the Teutoburg Forest!) of course through their reading of Roman classics, especially Tacitus, whom the humanists revered. From the Roman origins of Germany also sprang the "typically German" anti-Roman sentiment which just as deeply entangled this country in an odd love-hate relationship and caused the Church and Europe to break apart into two pieces centuries ago.

However let us start again at the beginning. Back to the stone which, as an almost forgotten path marker on the floor of Saint Peter's Basilica, commemorates one of the most important turning points in the history of Europe. Day after day, thousands of gaping German pilgrims and tourists who have no idea

whatsoever of this history walk through Saint Peter's Basilica
right over it. But of course most of the Franks were not able to
interpret the epochal change of the year 800 either until centuries later. In what should probably be understood as a similar but
much more sublime step, Joseph Ratzinger one year ago appeared
on the *Loggia* over Saint Peter's Square as Pope Benedict XVI.
Coming after the great Pole in the shoes of the fisherman, the
turning point of this election was once again, from a historical
perspective as well, a very special sort of chess move by the Holy
Spirit. Not because, or not only because, this time a solitary
master thinker followed the prophetic John Paul II. The more
momentous fact was that on April 19, 2005, for the first time
a man from the land of the Reformation became the successor
of Peter. Since that evening Germany has had a new center of
gravity, far outside its boundaries, about 2,000 kilometers (1,240
miles) distant from Berlin — even though many or most Germans
in Germany perhaps notice that as little as the Franks at the time
of Charlemagne's coronation in Rome understood that epochal
change. How could it be otherwise?

Things look different in Rome, however, where the Romans
found Benedict XVI "*dolce*" [charming] from day one — and soon
afterward revered a "Thomas Aquinas of our time" on the papal
throne. One year later, though, Rome itself has now become
again a city of German voices: almost a "Rome of the German
Nation." On a normal day Benedict XVI draws far more pilgrims
than his great predecessor to every Wednesday audience, to every
Angelus at noon on Sunday, when Saint Peter's Square is bursting at the seams, even in winter.

Therefore he was right on April 19, 2005, when he saw the
vote of the cardinals coming toward him "like the blade of a
guillotine." The subsequent election in fact separated his entire

former life from him in a split second—but it also separated one epoch from another. Since that day, in secularized Europe, there have again been two authorities, at least equal in rank, for interpreting society, politics, history, and ethics. Since that cool April day the primacy of an often totalitarian secular worldview collapsed like a house of cards under a light drizzle on Saint Peter's Square. In the midst of the radical change in values, no one disputes the equal entitlement of Benedict XVI to speak in all relevant debates. Perhaps more decisive for Germany, nevertheless, is one little detail: after the horrible trials and experiences of the last "German" century, it was summed up most ingeniously in the headline of the *Bild* newspaper: *"Wir sind Papst"*—"We are Pope." For it is in fact true: Since April 19, 2005, German Lutherans have "their" Pope too, and German Evangelicals as well as German Jews, German Muslims, German agnostics, and even German atheists and neo-pagans—and last but not least German Catholics, so many of whom so often, faced with the battles over faith in the last century, had hung a sort of modernity around their necks that made them seem hopelessly old and old-fashioned the very next day. With the first step of Benedict XVI over the threshold of the Sistine Chapel the German hour of the Universal Church had begun.

And yet: It remains an hour of history, an allotted interval of time, a unique opportunity, and probably not an era. No one will be more aware of this than Benedict XVI himself, and he will know how to make use of the time—at an age, of course, that distinguishes him only a little from his predecessor. He no longer has much time, observers might think. Yet he had his red chasuble embroidered all over with the scallop shell from his coat of arms, just like the Bourbon kings once decorated their mantles with the lilies of the field from the Sea of Gennesaret.

Benedict Up Close

The scallop is the symbol of Saint Augustine's search for truth, as well as the distinctive badge of the pilgrims to Santiago. Benedict XVI intends to keep walking a bit farther. He has three goals firmly in mind even now. He will defend the sanctity of the human person against any ideology. His predecessor had suffered under totalitarianism. He, though, experienced "the totalitarian temptation" close up as a German, whereas the younger generations have hardly any idea of its dangers. Moreover he will restore the liturgy as the sacred space, since he experienced its breakdown as though it were a cathedral caving in. The Council left breaches behind in the Church like an earthquake, and he will carefully try to bridge the gaps. Finally he will no longer shirk the Christian duty to defend the Church's claims in the public arena—bringing the Church out of the private niche into which Europe's Christians for centuries have let themselves be driven. A lost cause? Maybe. He will nevertheless take it up. In him modernity as well as the "dictatorship of relativism" is confronted with a champion of the absolute, who justified his motto ("Co-workers of the Truth") as early as 1977 in these words: "because in today's world the topic of truth has almost completely disappeared, because it appears to be too big for man, and yet everything falls apart if there is no truth."

Thus Benedict XVI has even now reconnected Germany with Rome and Rome with Germany: in an exciting connection of origins. His predecessor brought Poland back onto the world map. But he has brought Rome back onto the German map. Back to the Germans, among whom the Roman element—whether loved or hated—has embodied all along the universal and global elements of their identity. In an ironic coincidence, Rome in the age of globalization thus comes back to Germany as the one that is suddenly more modern.

From Krakow to Auschwitz — Krakow, May 28, 2006

Rain is pattering. The blare of a trumpet goes over the roofs of Krakow, very faintly. The watchman can scarcely be heard as he sounds the hour to all four points of the compass from the steeple of Saint Mary's Basilica. It poured already in Warsaw, and now again for half a night in the South of Poland. Saint Peter dreamed up for the trip of his 264th successor weather that you would not send a dog out into. It is cold. Yet hundreds of thousands have streamed to Krakow in the rain: children, young people, and old, often with a priest in the lead, usually in a cassock, with backpacks and sleeping bags on their backs. Have they come from another planet? Yes, Benedict XVI has traveled to the "distant land" from which John Paul II came, before he led it back into the round-dance [*Reigen*] of the free peoples of Europe. He walks in his footsteps, he arrives on his shoulders, "overcome by feelings," yet not on a "sentimental journey."

He preaches on the same public squares, stands at the same windows, prayed in his place, visits his favorite shrines, kneels at the grave of Jan Sobieski, the liberator of Vienna from the menacing Turkish threat. In Karol Wojtyła's birthplace he quotes Goethe: "Whoever wants to understand a poet should take a look at his native place." The thinker from Germany wants to understand the poet from Poland. Here he wants to comprehend better the man who in Rome sat right in front of him on the papal throne.

The teacher came as a learner, and Poland came to meet him with lessons that not even the Vatican can offer. Compared with this country, Catholic Italy resembles a Communist republic of freethinkers. Like John Paul II, Poland too is a special case in history, being Europe's last heroic nation. Since Thursday it has been meeting with the Pope from the land of Luther, once again as the bulwark against which the Soviet system finally ran aground: against a nation on its knees, against a police cordon made out of rosaries, which until now has neither torn nor been laid down. In front of the Shrine in Częstochowa the prayer beads were in practically every hand. Near the Black Madonna on the White Mountain, near the "Queen of Poland," the sun broke through the cloud cover again, as Benedict XVI met there with Poland's priests, nuns, monks, and seminarians, who since the reign of John Paul II have sprung up from the land as nowhere else in Europe. Vocations are exploding like the chestnut blossoms this May. For a long time now Poland has been exporting them to the Universal Church. The pontificate of John Paul II was "not an ethnic oddity," the American papal biographer George Weigel from Washington wrote recently in Poland's major newspaper *Dziennek*, but rather was stamped by a particular national and cultural experience that is of universal significance for the Church throughout the world. John Paul II already had a vision that Poland would assume an altogether key role in bringing Europe to a rebirth of freedom that would help the old West out of its deep crisis. He regarded Poland as a laboratory of the Catholic Church. Benedict XVI at any rate has traveled here even before he undertakes his trip back home to Bavaria. The country charms him, and he charms the Poles, as noble as a fairytale king in his red, ermine-lined mozetta [cape]. He laughs. He smiles. Cardinal Dziwisz, the former secretary of John Paul II, suddenly stands at his side as though in a déjà-vu. And on Saturday, when he bows to the rejoicing young people in Błonie Park like Mahatma Gandhi, the farmer from Marktl am Inn has suddenly become a Pole himself. On Sunday afternoon he exclaims to the gigantic crowd of people at that same place: "Krakow, the city of Karol Wojtyła and John Paul II, is also my

Krakow!" Yes, with this journey Poland has in fact become his Poland too. At his departure he asks them courageously "to share the treasure of the faith with the other peoples of Europe and of the world." The whole nation should now follow the personal example of John Paul II. Afterward the heavens over Krakow are rent.

Nevertheless, it is not farewell yet. Four hours after reminding the people in Błonie Park that "the Creator has placed us on this earth as the crown of His work of creation," he goes to the place "as a son of the German people" who "could not fail to come." From Krakow the pilgrim from Rome travels to Auschwitz and Birkenau, the names of which Germans once branded onto the map of the country like brand marks on cattle: as worlds of horror, eternally connected with the "mystery of evil" that his predecessor recalled again and again in bewilderment. "Death," the "Master from Germany" that once ruled here, is followed today by the Pope who comes from Germany.

Over 4,000 journalists obtained credentials in order to cover the high-wire act: the German voice of the Successor of Peter about the abyss of nihilism that yawned here under a German name. Isn't he bound to fall? Over landscapes made up of mountains of eyeglasses and ravines of shoes, over the blown-up chimneys of these ruins arches a "grave in the atmosphere" for millions in the heights. The white birch trunks of Birkenau sway and bend and dance in the wind, May-green. Between the trees a glimmering pond, its bottom rich with human ashes, among them the remains of the "Doctor of the Church" Teresa Benedicta of the Cross, a "daughter of Israel and daughter of the Church," as John Paul II called her — who as the Jewess Edith Stein was gassed and incinerated here, and her ashes had a damp burial in the pond with those of countless others. Glints of sunlight are reflected on the black surface. Leaves drift back and forth on the water. Then it rains again. In the last weeks of her life Edith Stein would still have gladly emigrated to Jerusalem. Yet Birkenau became her destiny.

"To speak in this place of horror, in this place where unprecedented mass crimes were committed against God and man, is almost impossible," the Pope says right at the beginning. Yet he must speak, even though he invokes silence and cries out to God with the Psalmist: "Rise up, come to our help! . . . Awake, do not cast us off forever!" He comes here in the sight of God and of the world as a "son of that people" which had fallen into the hands of "criminals [who] rose to power by false promises"; "those vicious criminals, by wiping out this people [of Israel], wanted to kill the God who called Abraham, who spoke on Sinai and laid down principles to serve as a guide for mankind. . . . That God finally had to die and power had to belong to man alone — to those men who thought that by force they had made themselves masters of the world."

From here, though, he calls to God also in our present hour, "when new misfortunes befall us, when all the forces of darkness seem to issue anew from human hearts: whether it is the abuse of God's name as a means of justifying senseless violence against innocent persons, or the cynicism which refuses to acknowledge God and ridicules faith in him." May God finally help mankind realize "that violence does not bring peace, but only generates more violence — a morass of devastation in which everyone is ultimately the loser." Finally he invokes over the world of horror the "star of reconciliation." Here over this darkness this star first arose between the German and the Polish Bishops — at the place where the Catholic Pontiff now begs the world in the words of the pagan Sophocles: "My nature is not to join in hate but to join in love"—while the heavens finally open entirely over Birkenau and a faint rainbow surrounds the "grave in the atmosphere" like a halo.

The return of Veronica — Rome, August 30, 2006

Mankind has lost a face, an irretrievable face, and all have longed to be that pilgrim ... who in Rome sees the veil of Veronica and murmurs in faith, "Lord Jesus, my God, true God, is this then what Thy face was like?"

—Jorge Luis Borges, *Dreamtigers*, 1960

Eastern Christendom celebrates an "image made by God" every year on August 16. Corresponding in the West to the feast of the "*Hagion Mandylion*" [the Holy Facecloth] is the Veronica pillar in Saint Peter's Basilica. The first pillar beneath the dome of Saint Peter's was constructed by Popes Julius II through Urban VIII as a vault for the so-called Jerusalem Facecloth of Veronica. Yet neither in the East nor in the West is there today such a "true image," a *vera ikon*, and it is quite odd that this has not surprised anyone for a long time. For centuries the miraculous original image of Christ has simply no longer been on our radar screens. In the year 1475 it still appeared as the true coat of arms of Christian Rome over the papal insignia. The precious relic drew millions of pilgrims. On a magnificent flag that Julius II entrusted to the Swiss Guard in 1512, the mysterious image on the veil is suspended over the keys of Peter. It was the treasure that members of the Guard had to protect above all, besides the Pope. One hundred forty of them heroically allowed themselves to be mowed down for Pope Clement VII fifteen years later, when Spanish and German mercenaries ravaged the Eternal City in the "*Sacco di Roma*." The Pope escaped to Castel Sant'Angelo. Shortly afterward "the Veronica passed from hand to hand through the catacombs of Rome," it says in an old document. In Saint Peter's Basilica, however, the image continued to be exhibited, but less and less often—and only from a distance. Copies of the "true image" continued to circulate too. They showed the Face of Christ, but soon only with his eyes closed, whereas before they had always been open.

So the original image did not simply disappear; it trickled away. The loss was ingeniously hushed up. For the intellectual history of Europe, nevertheless, the process became a watershed, after which the notion that there is a real original measure for all Christian art was lost in an almost ghostly amnesia of Christianity. Now a similar paradigm shift is being heralded today by the journey of Benedict XVI to Manoppello. For in that little village in Abruzzi a veil with an image has been preserved for centuries; some years ago Professor Heinrich Pfeiffer from the Gregorian University, a German, discovered on it all the characteristics with which the "true image" in Rome was depicted in old sources.

From both sides of the cloth, the Face of Christ looks at us; the theologian Bruno Forte says that "it unites pain and light in itself as closely as only love can." There are other "holy faces" in Italy. Yet in comparison with them the veil-icon in Manoppello appears to be from another planet. If a Renaissance master had painted it, for instance Dürer or Leonardo da Vinci, art lovers from all the corners of the earth would have to make the pilgrimage to Abruzzi on their knees. If instead it is the old Veronica, then the time of its origin also immediately jumps back to the year 704. From that point in time on there are records of the "Facecloth" in Rome—and there, in the context of the Carolingian and also Byzantine world of images, it defies all comparison.

The face curves toward the viewer. In an illuminated manuscript of Dante's *Divine Comedy* from the year 1390 we encounter the same inexplicable face as though on an arrest warrant, with a host of angels fluttering around it. Here, in the *Divine Comedy*, Benedict XVI himself already rediscovered the face months ago (in Canto 33, verses 130-132). Three visionary lines in it inspired him to write his first Encyclical about the God of love. Since then he has continued to write a "theological narrative" about "Christ as the living icon of God." With regard to the image of God in the religions of the book, nevertheless, his journey today is perhaps talked about more than any text. In a world dominated by images, his very arrival is more eloquent than the rustling of pages in any library. Even before the rotors of the helicopter start up to take him back to Castel Gandolfo, the Pope has catapulted the silent face on the veil in Manoppello to the attention of the whole world on this Friday. In the incredible story about the return of the Veronica he now opens a new chapter in which the "true image" is being discussed as it had not been in four hundred years.

"Then Simon Peter came ... and saw ... the napkin, which had been on his head." Archbishop Forte wrote this verse from the Resurrection account of John in Greek on the edge of an icon of Christ that he gave the Successor of Peter today as a present. The erudite Chief Shepherd of Chieti is convinced "with moral certainty" that the "Holy Face" of Manoppello originally came from the empty tomb of Christ. Thus the delicate cloth by its very existence calls into question large sections of contemporary theology. For the modern spirit of the age within and outside of Christianity, such an object, of course, cannot exist at all.

The background for all the controversy about the cloth therefore has beyond the Pope's visit an ontological dimension.

Is it a miracle? Is it the napkin or facecloth that John spoke about? Is it the true image? No Pope can answer that question casually. Even the inhabitants of Manoppello have hardly believed that in the last four hundred years. The only indubitable thing is that for a long time there was a tradition in Christianity that started from the rock-solid belief in the existence of such a true image of Christ on a veil. The image in Manoppello, however inexplicable it may be, corresponds to this tradition. It shows the Word made flesh. Benedict XVI cannot view it without emotion. As a Cardinal he already learned: However old a lie may be, the truth is even older. The truth precedes any deception. A lie is always fabricated. Truth is.

"Viewers do not look for their icons," they say in the East, "but icons look for their viewers." If that is true, then the "Holy Face" has now sought Benedict XVI himself. His predecessor Benedict XIV approved the miracle of Our Lady of Guadalupe in Mexico in 1754 for the Catholic Church with the Brief *Non est quidem*. Benedict XVI, however, will approve and recognize the Face of Manoppello in his own way. "One does not see the Risen Lord like a piece of wood or stone," Joseph Ratzinger wrote in 1985. "He is seen only by those to whom He reveals Himself. And He reveals Himself only to someone whom He can send. He reveals Himself not to curiosity but to love."

Cosmic Excursion (Jesus and Peter) —
Manoppello, September 1, 2006

At three o'clock in the night human voices in the valleys and ravines around Manoppello awaken us, an hour when usually the barking of dogs starts and in winter sometimes the howling of wolves. The dogs are quiet right now. The pilgrims are coming already in the middle of the night. Around five the tramping of their feet around the rural hotel recalls those days after the death of John Paul II, as the stream of mourners in the streets of Rome swelled to a cosmic Love Parade. Today Benedict XVI comes for a "cosmic excursion" to the Abruzzi region, to the little shrine above the hotel, in order to look at the human face in which Dante recognized the Face of God in the year 1320 — in the midst of a threefold circle of light and love that "moves the sun and the stars." Today the visit of the Successor of Peter moves the inhabitants of Abruzzi. But far from all of them can come. The ability of the little village to accommodate them is much too limited. The narrow streets are blocked off in a wide surrounding area. The infrastructure of the forgotten hills and valleys in front of the Majella massif is totally overstrained by the event. Only 8,000 tickets were issued to selected participants to welcome the Pope on the square in front of the little Capuchin church — on average one for each family in the vicinity. Most people have to follow the event on television or on a jumbo screen down on the via Tiburtina. Today only priests, nuns, and monks are allowed into the church of the "Holy Face." The sky however stretches as spotlessly blue over Manoppello on this first September morning as if the day had been prescribed in Paradise. For centuries the little locality has preserved a veil with the "Holy Face" in which Capuchin Father Domenico da Cese discovered decades ago the napkin from Jerusalem that the Evangelist John speaks about in his account of Christ's Resurrection.

The inhabitants of Manoppello have him above all to thank for the fact that the Pope is seeking out this marvelous and equally secluded corner of Italy today. In Rome the discovery long ago stirred up heated debates. No Pope could settle all the questions that have meanwhile been raised about the authenticity of the image. Consequently there was staunch opposition to this "private" pilgrimage by the Pope even in the highest ranks of the Curia. Yet Benedict XVI insisted on taking a look at the image himself now.

A crimson mozetta is draped over the Pope's shoulders. He is glad to see "all these faces," he calls to the inhabitants of Manoppello as he turns around in the open church door toward the crowd of people who have gathered in front of it. Then he walks forward with his entourage into the church building (where over the tabernacle on the main altar the veil shines with a milky glow from a back-lit monstrance) and goes down on his knees before the tabernacle, the Holy of Holies of every Catholic church, casts his eyes downward, prays, keeps his eyes closed, finally opens them, and looks up to the little veil above. Slow motion. Silence. Somewhere a camera whirrs. A cough in the back of the church. Then finally he stands up, starts to turn to the left but goes to the right. Archbishop Forte guides him up a stairway behind the altar. The glass window of the vault that usually protects the miraculous image from pilgrims and thieves is now folded back.

At the top of the stairs the Pope folds his hands and just looks. His fingers intertwined. Motionless. As serious as in Auschwitz, as deep in thought as his predecessor on Golgotha, with eyes wide open, silent, looking, one minute, two, three, four, an eternity. Again and again a choir of seminarians sings a song by the Little Flower, Thérèse of Lisieux, the Saint "of the Holy Face," that praises the beauty of Jesus' Face, which "carried her heart away": "O *Volto Santo di Gesù....*" The Pope looks. The bishop on his left invites him to come down again. He waves him off with his right hand, enthralled. Are his lips moving? He stands upright, alert, silent. Finally he makes the Sign of the Cross over himself, carefully goes down the steps, then back to the altar and begins to speak: "During my pause for prayer just now, I was thinking of the first two Apostles who, urged by John the Baptist, followed Jesus to the banks of the Jordan River... [and asked,] 'Rabbi, where are you staying?' And he said to them, 'Come and see.' That very same day, the two who were following him had an unforgettable experience which prompted them to say: 'We have found the Messiah.'" Suddenly they had recognized the true identity of the one whom they had formerly perceived merely as teacher and rabbi. And nevertheless: How much longer would they have to follow Him until His unfathomable Face would be truly unveiled to them? "He who sees me, sees the Father," they had learned from Him. Yet they would realize it only when they met the Risen Lord and "the Spirit enlightened their minds and their hearts." Someone who in this holy tradition "lives in God already on this earth, attracted and transformed by the dazzling brightness of His Face," will recognize His Face again and again, "especially in the poorest and neediest." That is the teaching of the saints who again and again have shed new light of the Face of Christ.

Sister Blandina Paschalis Schlömer looks at him, speechless. Countless times this German Trappist nun put a transparency of this Holy Face on the face on the Shroud of Turin and on the noblest depictions of Christ in art history and thus startled the academic world. There is nothing that she wishes more than to see the Pope bless the world with the monstrance of the Holy Face. He however now places the transparency of the Holy Face on the faces of all mankind. "May the Lord help you more and more to recognize His Face, so as to see the Father. In union of prayers and in our common search for His Face — Benedict XVI. September 1, 2006," the Pope writes to the Capuchins afterward in the guest book in the sacristy, after he dismissed everyone with the blessing of ancient Israel: "The LORD bless you and keep you: The LORD make His face to shine upon you. . . . The LORD lift up His countenance upon you, and give you peace."

"The Pope was enthusiastic!" Archbishop Forte exclaims in German in the throng in front of the church door when Benedict XVI is airborne again and he himself is being led away to a press conference. The Pope's comment on the Holy Face was above all "his silent prayer," he says afterward to the worldwide press. What remains are the empty water bottles on the streets and among them a few song sheets that Archbishop Forte had printed for this day. His friend Luciano Primavera designed them. The heading shows in a red pencil drawing the image that this day will impress on the memory of history. It could be a dream of Sister Blandina. In it Benedict XVI lifts the veil showing the image of the Holy Face with both hands over his head toward the world as a blessing. Jesus and Peter. Both are relaxed, composed, smiling.

New Seal — Rome, September 8, 2006

Joseph Ratzinger began his career as a pastor as a skeptic. Thirty years ago the new Chief Shepherd of more than a billion Catholics was not even certain whether in his lifetime he might not have to witness the total de-Christianization of Bavaria. In 1977, when he became Archbishop of Munich and Freising, in what was then and is now the most Catholic part of Germany, he had a rather gloomy view of the future. Three decades since then have taught him otherwise in many respects. Not that the times have improved meanwhile by becoming more peaceful, more conciliatory, or even more Christian. But Joseph Ratzinger's view has broadened immensely once again in the eyes of Benedict XVI. As

Bishop of Rome and of the Universal Church he returns today to his old home, not exactly as an optimist, but nevertheless decisively more hopeful.

Before his departure he wished a "springtime of faith" for the country in which Karl Rahner in his day had coined the phrase and the image of a "wintry Church." "Just look at that! Look across to the bank," Cardinal Meisner said to him last August on the Rhine in Cologne, pointing to the young people who were standing up to their knees in the water, as if it were the Ganges. "Just look at that. Here you do not always have to speak, you must wave to them." The new Pontiff defensively asked him, please, not to boss him around like that. "Nonsense, Holy Father!" came the reply, "You are so intelligent, you can easily learn that too even at your age." Meisner was right. In the last sixteen months the master thinker at an advanced age has learned once again as an apprentice "the craft" of being Pope, as he himself describes it. It was a crash course, in which he made almost no mistakes, except — perhaps — at his first public Angelus prayer, which he still began with the words: "*Carissimi fratelli e sorelle,*" "Dearest brothers and sisters!" Then he too realized that in his lifetime this formula would always remain a trademark of his "beloved predecessor": to this day, whenever he mentions him publicly, he is interrupted with applause. Since then Benedict XVI goes to the window every Sunday with the words: "*Cari fratelli e sorelle* — Dear brothers and sisters!" He is more objective, no less cordial. Nevertheless, he draws to Rome time after time more pilgrimages than the great, charismatic John Paul II. In Munich too now he will draw no fewer people.

The skeptic is still there in Benedict XVI, as though in a Russian *matryoshka* doll: the enigmatic fan of the Bavarian comedian

Karl Valentin, the old Joseph Ratzinger with his weakness for dry irony that is often distinguished from mockery only by nuances. And how could it be otherwise? He worked at various professions; now he is working at his final one, this time as a definitive calling, but still with the same sober passion with which he learned in Precious Blood parish in Munich-Bogenhausen more than fifty years ago "how to bury." At a recent Symposium in Castel Gandolfo on the topic of "Creation and Evolution" there an important paper was read by the philosopher Robert Spaemann, who prefaced the discussion of the scientists, philosophers, and theologians in their inquiry into the origin of all life with a motto taken from Friedrich Schiller:

> *Feindschaft sei zwischen euch, noch kommt das*
> *Bündnis zu frühe.*
> *Wenn ihr im Suchen euch trennt, wird erst die*
> *Wahrheit erkannt.*
> Let there be enmity between you; for agreement
> it is still too early.
> Only if you separate while searching will the
> truth be known.

It was a statement quite to the taste of Joseph Ratzinger and Benedict XVI. For the search for truth tolerates not only reconciliation. Ratzinger and Benedict XVI are not Jekyll and Hyde. Nor is the Pope a butterfly that was once a caterpillar. The one nevertheless matured into the other. Then too, in the breast of the Successor of Peter still beats the heart of a professor who loves intricate questions and intellectual challenges, and he considers them as a chess player does his next unexpected move. He is always a good one for surprises, on his trip through Bavaria too. He will dazzle again with surprising steps and trains of thought. This way of moving others has long since become second nature to him.

Nevertheless, to regard the Pope from Germany as a former intellectual is to understand less than half of the man. Every Wednesday he takes his place in front of Saint Peter's Basilica as an ecclesiastical teacher. Teaching is an old passion of his, yet he gets more attention nowadays for the messages that he delivers in an entirely new language that you can observe him learning week by week. It is not the difficult Polish language that he is learning for the sake of his predecessor. For the sake of the whole world, in addition to the ancient and modern languages that he has mastered so far, he is now acquiring also a new language of signs, which previously never played this role in his life. It is the art of the semantics of signals and gestures, of leaving out and adding to, in which he has already become a master.

Last year he still used to wave to the pilgrims at Castel Gandolfo Sunday after Sunday with the hands of a pianist or a puppeteer, with dancing fingers, as though he wanted to call them up individually to himself. Those hands have calmed down since then. Ever since the viewfinders of the cameras have been firmly set on him, he has however not ceased to play with new signals, as it were: for instance with the "*camauro*" in the early months of this year, the old fur-lined cap of the Medici popes, or the "*saturno*," a crimson summer hat with which he won countless front-page stories on Wednesday. It is a special cheerfulness with which he is able to charm today, whereas earlier he knew how to move almost invisibly in the lanes of the Borgo in front of the Vatican.

Against the background of this cheerfulness, the erudite polyglot is able now to speak in silence in an especially unsettling way, while abandoning all language, by peering earnestly, in silent prayer—like John Paul II. He spoke most clearly in Auschwitz in this way, and so he spoke in Spain—and finally just last week in a little village in the Abruzzi, as over 600 journalists accompanied him to an allegedly "controversial" relic, only to observe there how he simply abided in silence before the enigmatic image of Christ and allowed himself to be deeply moved by its gaze. An untold number of words had been used in countless editors' offices, beforehand about all sorts of things that he would not actually say, and afterward about what he had not said. He however just stood there and looked, a shepherd before the crib, in amazed disbelief, while he very quietly catapulted the ancient face of Christ and an awareness of Christianity back to all the corners of the earth via satellite: the living image of God among all religions.

Words about it did not fail him. "To express ourselves in accordance with the paradox of the Incarnation we can certainly say that God gave Himself a human Face," he informed the participants in his General Audience the preceding Wednesday. It is "the Face of Jesus, and consequently, from now on, if we truly want to know the Face of God, all we have to do is to contemplate the Face of Jesus! In His Face we truly see who God is and what He looks like!" Joseph Ratzinger always wanted to enhance the profile of Christians. Now as Pope, he instead makes looking at the human Face of God the hallmark of his pontificate.

Preaching penance to modernity:
A departure—Munich, September 10, 2006

The heavens are whitish-blue. The weather—spectacular. Bavaria as in a picture book. Cirrus clouds sketch puzzling signs high in the sky. For decades Munich's old airport was located at the present site of the *Neue Messe*, the city's convention center.

As a Cardinal, Joseph Ratzinger departed many times from here on flights to Rome. Many times he arrived back on the open area in front of the city gates, where as Pope he celebrated his first Mass in Bavaria. Today Benedict XVI is not taking off. The policeman's son from the *Académie française* on the Throne of Peter is not triumphing either. Nevertheless, it is a triumphal return for someone who formerly could not even obtain honorary citizenship in Munich. *Tempi passati!* [Let bygones be bygones!] Now the new mayor of this city on the Isar and the old ones are waiting in line, behind the President and the Federal Chancellor, so as to be able to extend their hands in welcome to the monarch of the Vatican mini-state.

He is returning to Munich for a "feast of faith," the Pope said in the airplane. There he wants to present the Church anew as a mighty "force of peace." The play of expressions on his face, his gestures, his smile, and all his words nevertheless also betray the fact that he is quite simply happy about this trip. The evening before, at the Marian Pillar, light fell on him like a shining shadow. The hands on the tower clock of the Cathedral of Our Lady gleamed like gold in the evening sunlight, and as the choir singing the Bavarian anthem finally arrived at the refrain: "*Gott mit dir, du Land der Bayern, unterm Himmel weiss und blau*" ["God be with you, O land of the Bavarians, under the white-and-blue sky"], just then a single aircraft beneath the radiant blue heavens drew a snow-white trail of condensation diagonally over the square. Right here, on this spot, Joseph Ratzinger had also departed from Munich on February 28, 1982, after John Paul II called him to Rome to head the Congregation for the Doctrine of the Faith.

He was never estranged from his origins, however. With this journey he wanted to return home once again, he said this time at his departure, and to see again gratefully the places and people who had formed him—or their graves. He is "an old man" who after this visit could regard any further trip to Germany only as a "gift" that for the time being he himself could no longer plan. "As the Pope of the Universal Church" he must give priority now to preparations for his journey "to Constantinople and Brazil."

One single snow-white cloud has settled high up in the sky over the altar island like a skull cap as the Pontiff arrives at the site for the Mass. Drum rolls accompany him as he rides in through the crowd, with flags fluttering as on Saint Peter's Square. Tens of thousands streamed into the former airport site during the night. Cardinal Wetter, his host, had the Enghausen Cross brought from a suburb of Munich as the only decoration behind the altar; the restoration team only recently found out that it is the oldest life-size crucifix in the world: a major work of sculpture more than eleven hundred years old, in which Christ on the Cross wears no crown of thorns, but looks at the viewer with wide-open, big blue eyes, with His mouth slightly open as though he were about to breathe on each one. It is a treasure of the diocese that not even the Pope himself had recognized or been acquainted with when he was still Archbishop in Munich and Freising.

A Polish colleague [of the author] claims to have detected "a bombshell" in the text of his homily, and over the news ticker of the Italian newspaper *Corriere della Sera* an urgent report travels over the Internet that the West is afraid of Islam—although the word "Islam" appears nowhere in the manuscript of the papal homily. Nevertheless, the interpretation is not wrong, but that is due rather to the real bombshells of our age. "Then Jesus returned from the region of Tyre, and went through Sidon to the Sea of Galilee," the Gospel of the day begins, with the names of the cities that a few weeks ago became the scene of bloody, horrible battles. In recent days he let every visitor know how much the situation in the Holy Land and the Near East fills him with grief.

The peoples of Africa and Asia, he now exclaims, "admire, indeed, the scientific and technical prowess of the West, but they are frightened by a form of rationality which totally excludes God from man's vision, as if this were the highest form of reason, and one to be taught to their cultures too." These nations do not see the Christian faith as the real threat to their identity, but rather contempt of God and the cynicism that regards mockery of what is sacred as a free right and takes what is useful for the future successes of research as the ultimate standard. "Dear friends," he exclaims urgently, "this cynicism is not the kind of tolerance and cultural openness that the world's peoples are looking for and that all of us want! The tolerance which we urgently need includes the fear of God — respect for what others hold sacred. This respect for what others hold sacred demands that we ourselves learn once more the fear of God."

Applause interrupts him. At the beginning of his trip home to this "feast of faith" the friendly, happy Pope also lamented a "hardness of hearing where God is concerned, . . . from which we particularly suffer in our own time. Put simply, we are no longer able to hear God — there are too many different frequencies filling our ears." In this background noise, whatever is said about God seems pre-scientific. "This weakening of our capacity for perception drastically and dangerously curtails the range of our relationship with reality in general. The horizon of our life is disturbingly foreshortened." It is as if Joseph Ratzinger on this radiant September day had returned once more as Abraham a Santa Clara to the strongholds of the "dictatorship of relativism": an undaunted preacher of penance to the post-modern world.

Yet the Pope comes to the heart of his speech only when he outlines concretely the profile of any Christian "force of peace," which Christians owe to their experiences with the personal God, without which the freedom of the Western world is unthinkable. Faith therefore can occur only in freedom. "We do appeal to the freedom of men and women to open their hearts to God, to seek him, to hear his voice." For the world needs God, he says gently in his concluding plea. "We need God. But what God do we need? In the first reading, the prophet tells a people suffering oppression that: 'He will come with vengeance' [Isaiah 35:4]. We can easily suppose how the people imagined that vengeance. But the prophet himself goes on to reveal what it really is: the healing goodness of God. And the definitive explanation of the prophet's word is to be found in the one who died for us on the Cross: in Jesus, the Son of God incarnate."

At this point the Pope leaves his prepared text and points to the ancient cross at his back, "to the Son of God made man, who so impressively looks at us here." The face looks out over him to the crowd in front of him; the cameras zoom in to both. "His 'vengeance' is the Cross: His no to violence, His 'love unto the end.' This is the God we need!"

From somewhere in the sky a dove has flown in and lands over the pierced right hand of the Crucified, as though it were a tree.

Mary, the Woman and Our Mother — *Altötting, September 11, 2006*

The Chapel of Grace in Altötting was the morning star in young Joseph Ratzinger's firmament. His parents took him there by the hand for the first time when he was a child. Later he steered the ship of his life through many storms by the gentle light of that little shrine. Now he had chosen the idyllic village in Upper Bavaria to celebrate here on Monday his papal program in contrast to all the observances designed to exorcise the September 11 terror attacks on New York. That may sound exaggerated, but it is not. There are few coincidences in the Catholic world. Pope Benedict XVI is especially aware of and familiar with even the smallest details of this symbolic language that the Catholic Church has developed in her liturgy over millennia. At the age of seven he witnessed in Altötting the canonization of Blessed Brother Konrad of Parzham. In the previous century the popular local saint had renounced a large inheritance so as to be able to devote himself entirely to the pilgrims to the shrine and their needs. Last year Brother Konrad's feast day on April 21 on the Church calendar dominated the week in which Cardinal Ratzinger was elected Pope. Now the Bishop of Passau had Brother Konrad's remains displayed in Baroque simplicity in a crystal sarcophagus beneath the altar on which Pope Benedict celebrated Mass on Monday morning.

This event was not worth a single minute of air time for the American television networks, nor was the Pope's trip to Germany as a whole. "They couldn't care less," an American journalist later said about her editors back home in New York to her colleagues in the press center in Altötting, which had a view of the late summer day, of the Chapel of Grace and the jubilant crowd as the bell named "Heaven-stormer" [*die Stürmerin*] tolled in the bell tower and the brass bands started on the square.

The Pope, in contrast, does care to emphasize his own hierarchy of what is important in the rush of memories. Not a word about the falling towers in Manhattan, not a word about terror and the war against terror. Benedict XVI counters the horrors of September 11 with the little chapel of a shrine in his favorite place in his native Bavaria.

In front of the Black Madonna of Altötting, the "Mozart of theology" remembers the children's songs of Mother Church — and those of his own mother. He has devoted this entire day to just one woman: Mary, Miriam or Maryam, as the Muslims call the Blessed Virgin. Moreover during the Mass he explains the account of the miracle at the wedding feast of Cana, the first reported miracle of Jesus at a wedding feast in Galilee that was almost a failure. "It is worth listening to this Gospel reading for a deeper meaning," he says. It is worthwhile "so as to learn from Mary how to pray correctly. Mary actually makes no request of Jesus; she only says to him: 'They have no more wine.' Weddings in the Holy Land used to last a whole week; the whole village was involved, and so great quantities of wine were needed. Now the newlyweds are embarrassed, and Mary tells Jesus quite simply. She does not tell Jesus what he should do. She does not ask for anything in particular, certainly not that Jesus should perform a miracle by which He would produce wine. She simply entrusts the matter to Jesus and leaves it up to Him what He will do next. So we see two things in the simple words of the Mother of Jesus: on the one hand her loving care for people, the motherly alertness with which she notices other people's distress. We see her heartfelt kindness and her willingness to help. This is the mother to whom people have gone on pilgrimage to Altötting for generations. We entrust to her our cares, needs and troubles." He is the pilgrim Benedict, back in Altötting.

Yet then it is as though, in the land of the Reformation, he now wants to make Mary's beauty accessible to Lutheran Christians too — in one of those steps of reconciliation between the denominations that Federal President Köhler passionately requested of him for at his arrival. "Although in this way we can understand very well Mary's behavior and words, it is all the more difficult for us to understand Jesus' answer. Even the form of address seems unpleasant to us: 'Woman'—why does he not say 'Mother'? Well, this form of address expresses Mary's position in salvation history. It points ahead to the hour of the crucifixion, in which Jesus will say to her: 'Woman, behold your Son—Son, behold your mother.'" Thus it points ahead to the hour in which he will make the Woman, his Mother, the Mother of all disciples. And it refers back to the account of the creation of Eve: Adam saw himself as a human being alone in creation despite all its riches. Then Eve was created, and now he found the companion that he was waiting for, whom he named with the word 'woman.' Thus Mary is the new, definitive Woman in the Gospel of John, as the companion of the Redeemer, as our Mother: This apparently brusque answer expresses the greatness of her permanent mission." Benedict XVI sets this Woman and Mother in opposition to all the images of ghastly destruction that once again horrify and delight the world on this September 11, the bleak idol of the smoking towers.

Professor Pope—Regensburg, September 12, 2006

Rain beat against the cockpit of the Lufhansa jet as it landed at its destination on the return flight to the Roman Ciampino Airport. The Pope's journey to his country was a triumph. He seemed utterly blissful at the last stops. At the cathedral in Freising where he had been ordained, he set his prepared text aside and spoke as freely and animatedly as before. Now Vatican employees came to the gangway with big umbrellas to meet the Pope. Prelates whispered the latest news to the blissful Pontiff. The white-blue sky of Bavaria had been replaced by a heavy cloud cover over Latium [modern Lazio, the region of central western Italy]. An hour later it was pouring. Two hours later all the news tickers on all the major cable networks read: "Pope infuriates Muslim world"—"Pope's insults against the Qur'an cause uproar."

At the landing, no one on the plane could have known it. I looked out the window at the man in white as he disappeared among the cardinals and bishops in the terminal. A stressful week was coming to an end; yet it had rejuvenated him more and more from one day to the next. The film from last week was being replayed backwards. Once again I sat in the journalists' bus, which brought us through a Bavarian dream landscape from Munich to Regensburg. Early morning mist in the fields of hops. The sun over the hills and fields heavy with dew. The Pope's homeland. The well from which he had drawn water. It was difficult to concentrate on a new text that had been given out early that morning at around five in the Platzl Hotel.

It was not triumphalism, it was overwhelming joy in which Benedict had been swimming for three days like a fish in water. Never before had the world experienced a Benedict, aka Joseph Ratzinger, who was so relaxed, so much at home as here, where he tried to present the Church anew as a "force of peace." On Sunday a colleague had already recognized "a bomb" about Islam in the text of his homily. From the city of Lübeck a friend had phoned, telling about Muslims on the Baltic Sea who had exclaimed: "We have a Pope!"

Ratzinger's old adversary Hans Küng, in contrast, had been especially displeased with the appearance of the Lutheran Bishop of the Federal State of Bavaria, Johannes Friedrich, because he "was happy to have the privilege of giving a harmless sermon in the presence of the Pope." Friedrich had accompanied the

Pope to Altötting, to the Bavarian capital of Marian devotion in which he had never set foot until then, and had promised to come back again alone. Yet the ratings for the radio station *"Bayern 3"* [Bavaria 3], which was accompanying the Pope from morning until evening, were extremely high. Seventy percent of the listeners identified with him. Texts of homilies suddenly made front-page news. Since Boniface, it seemed, no one else had done missionary work in Germany except the first Pope from the land of the Reformation in recent days. In Altötting the pilgrim left his cardinal's ring at the feet of the "Queen of Peace" and "Comforter of the Afflicted."

The bus rolls on. I again take out the texts that he intends to read today, on Islinger Field before the gates of Regensburg, at the professorial chair of his old Alma Mater and in St. Peter's in Regensburg, a Gothic cathedral, at an ecumenical evening prayer service. "Faith is simple!" the old intellectual now in the shoes of the fisherman Peter intends to proclaim to the faithful in a few hours. Countless scholars had tried to find "an explanation of the world in which God would be unnecessary." Yet not one of them had got any farther than the alternative that boils down to the question: "What came first? Creative Reason, the Creator Spirit who makes all things and gives them growth, or Unreason, which, lacking any meaning, yet somehow brings forth a mathematically ordered cosmos, as well as man and his reason?" Nevertheless, precisely from this starting point the faith of Christians continues even more boldly. For they are convinced that creative Reason is Goodness: "It is Love. It has a face. God does not leave us groping in the dark. He has shown Himself to us as a man ... [and] has taken on a human face." Precisely now and today, when pathologies and life-threatening diseases of religion and of reason can be seen everywhere, along with the destruction of the image of God through hate and fanaticism, "it is important to state clearly the God in whom we believe, and to proclaim confidently that this God has a human face. Only this can free us from being afraid of God—which is ultimately the root of modern atheism."

This is his new *cantus firmus* [main theme or melody], and he gives variations on it at each stop on his journey. He had nothing else in mind but this new position statement of Catholic identity at his old Alma Mater, too, at the University of Regensburg, where the former professor now with one final farewell lecture wanted to be etched on the memory of his listeners and where his pedagogical love once again thrilled them as it had not done for a long time, as a souvenir of what was probably his favorite occupation. "Faith, Reason and the University" is the title of his "Reflections." The manuscript of the talk contained at the conclusion the note: "The Holy Father reserves the right to publish this text later with annotations. The present version should therefore be considered provisional."

Did he suspect how many annotations would be required? He will have to keep writing these annotations. It was the most complex text of his journey through Bavaria, in which he tried everywhere to explain his concern not to let himself and Catholic Christianity be co-opted in the culture wars, which he understands in a very particular way. The centers of conflict in the world cannot be classified according to a black-and-white scheme, he said time and again. The fronts run obscurely through all societies, in the West as in the East. After the age of the critique of God, it is urgent that the "reduction of the radius of science and reason" itself be called into question now. For "a reason which is deaf to the divine and which relegates religion into the realm of subcultures is incapable of entering into the dialogue of cultures." Like no one before him, he especially defended the Muslims too against unfettered secularism. Mohammedans probably have no better advocate today in the West than the Pope.

The peoples of Africa and Asia, he had said also on Sunday in Munich, "admire, indeed, the scientific and technical prowess of the West, but they are frightened by a form of rationality which totally excludes God from man's vision, as if this were the highest form of reason, and one to be taught to their cultures too.... The tolerance which we urgently need includes the fear of God — respect for what others hold sacred." He could not put it more clearly. Nevertheless, he did say the same thing in the Regensburg Address, probably in too complicated a way. The standing ovations could distract from it only for a short time.

For here the head of the Catholic Church had read several Surahs of the Qur'an too in a way that was as unabashedly text-critical as any theologian in the West has been doing for decades with the Bible. He took apart various strata of the text of the holy book when he said: "[In 1391] the [Byzantine] Emperor [Manuel II] must have known that Surah 2,256 reads: 'There is no compulsion in religion.' According to some of the experts, this is probably one of the surahs of the early period, when Mohammed was still powerless and under threat. But naturally the emperor also knew the instructions, developed later and recorded in the Qur'an, concerning holy war."

It was a minor, incidental aspect. The kindly professor-pope said something unheard-of softly, but it did not go unheeded. Marco Politi in *La Repubblica* called this breach of taboo "bizarre," and his colleague from *Il Corriere della Sera* joked that there might soon be a fatwa against the Pope. Philip Pullella from the Reuters news agency began his report with the words: "Pope Benedict invited Muslims to a dialogue of cultures, on the premise that the Islamic understanding of the 'holy war' is unreasonable and against the nature of God."

Spider webs glittered in the air. It was Joseph Ratzinger's last trip to the places where he was a child, a teacher and a bishop. From now on he was just the Pope. "Someone who reads the texts of his trip to Bavaria one after the other has in front of him an outline of the character that Benedict XVI wants his pontificate to have — except for the surprises which he probably will still be capable of. We can confidently understand the last days in his native country, however, as a sort of initial line of demarca-tion for his time in office — between his origins and the future [*Herkunft und Zukunft*]," I jotted in my notebook.

Yet it would have taken a Shakespeare to capture the cosmic drama that came crashing down on him upon his return to Rome with the delayed reaction to a few of his many words, at a water-shed of his pontificate. One day after his arrival in the worldwide uproar he commended unspecified "present difficulties" to Our Lady of Altötting as Advocate. Meanwhile the airspace over the papal summer residence in Castel Gandolfo was closed to any air traffic. Yet the following Sunday, in the pouring rain, he ap-peared again as nimble as a tightrope walker, in a raging storm. "I thank you all. You encourage me!" he called to the drenched pilgrims. For 2,000 years the Church had taught, one cartoonist in Rome joked earlier, "how to walk on eggs with leaden shoes." Now the Pope seemed to perform that feat successfully again.

His appearance was broadcast live by Al Jazeera to the Arab world. "It is raining a little," he said, laughing, as he looked up regretfully, "but we are strong." Then: "Hopefully the storm will let up soon." Moreover water is "a sign of the Holy Spirit." He stood at the window relaxed, with outspread arms, cheerful, free of anxiety, charming, full of sympathy. "I heartily regret the reactions that a few passages from my lecture at the University of Regensburg have elicited in some countries." Because Muslim believers had perceived the sentences as offensive, he had to emphasize once again that in fact they were nothing other than "quotations from a medieval document that in no way express my personal view." He smiled. His speech was, on the contrary, an invitation to an open, honest dialogue with great mutual respect. Then he turned to his prepared text—before beginning the Angelus, with that ancient dialogue between the Archangel Gabriel and the Virgin Mary, both of whom enjoy the utmost reverence in Islam. Now the prayer became a masterpiece of conflict management.

The Muslim Brotherhood had heard the words "with satisfaction," it was reported just minutes later from Egypt. They were "sufficient" as an apology. Religious war was dispelled. The cow appeared to be off the ice, if the comparison is permissible in this case, but from now on slick ice remains the ground on which Benedict has to learn again to walk. Once more the teacher had become the student. His last lecture had become for him an outstanding lesson—which will now be studied worldwide like none of his texts ever before. Overnight, however, the Successor of Peter has also become himself a leading figure of the Western world in the fire of the controversy. He will not let himself be turned into a champion marksman.

In the minefield of words—Castel Gandolfo, September 25, 2006

"*Gej iber Werter wi iber a Minenfeld,*" it says in a darkly humorous verse written by the Yiddish poet Abraham Sutzkever, after barely escaping the destruction of the Ghetto in Vilna. "Walk on words as though over a minefield." Should the head of Catholic

Christianity in our days perhaps have taken this advice to heart as he was composing his Regensburg lecture? Couldn't he have simply skipped over the improper quotation? It would hardly have been missed in the text as a whole. Maybe. But maybe not. Was it really a mistake to give a lecture so unguardedly and frankly as Benedict XVI did? The question has by no means been settled yet for the future. Certainly the Pope can neither have intended nor welcomed the deliberate exploitation of his words. The days afterward, however, offered him as never before an opportunity to present the specific features of a genuinely Christian attitude just as clearly to the world of Islam as to all his supposedly good advisers from the free world of the West. When so-called terrorism experts rushed afterward to the microphones to circulate among the people their analyses of the threat to the Vatican in general and to the Pope in particular, the Pontiff let himself be chauffeured around jam-packed Saint Peter's Square while standing in an open jeep with the windshield folded down. At the end of the week, after three Catholics in Indonesia were executed after an extremely dubious trial, he praised on Sunday at noon without any complaint the Italian nun Leonella Sgorbati, about whom witnesses testify that she died in Somalia speaking the word "forgiveness" as murderers gunned her down. Another part of this attempt at Christian self-definition and damage control is the Pope's meeting on Monday in Castel Gandolfo with representatives of the Muslim world, whom he amicably and resolutely reminded about religious freedom. His speech on the relation between religion, reason and violence has become, however, in the "House of Islam" as well as in the Western world, within just one week one of the most explosive documents of the century. Benedict XVI would never have wanted it that way and could never have wished it on himself. Nevertheless, even now his Regensburg Address has become one of the most significant documents of our era, the first "text of the century."

Back to the future—Rome, October 15, 2006

"Introibo ad altare Dei, ad Deum qui laetificat juventutem meam"—"I will go to the altar of God, the God who gives joy to my youth." When Benedict XVI was baptized, when he was an altar server, when he was ordained a priest, every Catholic Mass began with this fourth verse of Psalm 43 in Latin. It was the introductory formula of the Tridentine Rite of the Mass; it was the beginning of Catholic sacrificial liturgies, as they had developed over many centuries since the days of the early Christian community on Mount Zion in Jerusalem. Pius V had finally fixed the rite in a binding form "free of error" at the Council of Trent in the years 1545 and 1563. For four hundred years afterward this liturgy remained almost unchanged in the Catholic Church. It became part of the present Pope's flesh and blood from his earliest childhood.

If the custom were still in force, sextons might still have carried him after his election last year on a gestatorial chair to his coronation in Saint Peter's Basilica, walking behind an archdeacon who would have stopped the procession three times at appointed places and turned around, in order to burn a tuft of tow in a golden bowl with the admonishing words: *"Sancte Pater, sic transit gloria mundi!* (Holy Father, thus the glory of the world passes!)" But that was no longer how they did it, as everyone could see last year on television. Nor has the *Introibo* been recited at the beginning of every Catholic Mass for more than forty years—one of the countless innovations with which Catholic

Masses have been celebrated since the liturgical reform after the Second Vatican Council. For the Tridentine Rite with its obligatory Latin was abolished [*sic*] in 1969 during the pontificate of Paul VI and replaced with a new "Holy Mass in the Roman Rite," as the successor rite is officially called. In fact a radically changed form in the various vernacular languages is what followed the universally valid Sacrifice of the Mass in Latin.

Incredible hopes were set then on the introduction and implementation of the liturgical reform. It was a revolution to which only a few put up resistance at the start. It was therefore also a conflict that as early as the 1970's had led to the break with the French Archbishop Marcel Lefebvre, who did not want to abandon the old rite for anything in the world. The old celebration therefore survived afterward almost exclusively in a sort of Catholic underground—and in a few enclaves within the Church, for which exceptional permission had to be obtained from the local bishop, which was not always granted—far from it. Other absurdities in this policy elicited the anger and sharp-witted commentary of several Catholic intellectuals, among whom the philosopher Robert Spaemann and the writer Martin Mosebach played leading roles in Germany. Others could never silence their nagging doubts as to whether the reform had in fact proceeded too fast, too radically, and to some extent too arbitrarily—and whether it might not be substantially responsible for the erosion of the liturgy in general in recent decades: for the desacralization, de-divinization and trivialization of the way Catholic Masses are celebrated, which not only conservatives have noticed and deplored in many places.

For many years one of these skeptics had been Cardinal Ratzinger, who could be heard saying again and again that something that had grown could by no means be replaced simply by something "made" and that therefore a "reform of the reform" was perhaps necessary. At the turn of the millennium he devoted a critical book entirely to the endangered *Spirit of the Liturgy*. Nevertheless, a "reform of the reform" remains easier said than done. The reformers of 1969 claimed to be guided by the noble Latin rule of Saint Benedict: *"succisa virescit"* — "pruned back, it blooms again." The old liturgy, though, was hardly a vineyard that had run wild. The result, at any rate, stimulated not only a new flourishing and better fruits, but also unexpectedly new wild growth. Maybe the new liturgy really was "man-made" in many respects. For over forty years, however, it too has also "grown," luxuriantly and rankly, to the point of offering Clown Masses complete with putty noses, which certainly would have appalled the Fathers of the reform, but no longer surprises many Catholics, who have had to put up with it for so long now — if they have not entirely turned their backs on the Church because of such hullabaloo.

After the strict rubrics of the Tridentine Mass, the liturgical reform had made much more room for the subjective judgment of the celebrants — and thus had made Masses so to speak dependent on the talents of the priest or else on his lack of talent. Now there are signs of a decisive turning point in this development. According to reliable information from the Vatican, Benedict XVI will soon sign a document designed to allow the use of the Latin liturgy again worldwide without any restriction. According to this Decree there will continue to be only one rite in the Roman Catholic Church — from now on, however, with two equally entitled forms: the ordinary rite in the vernacular and the extraordinary and universal rite in Latin. Consequently the Pontiff is again granting to the old rite "full citizenship" in the Church of Rome. This is nothing less than the beginning of a cultural revolution. Nevertheless, this stroke of genius is not a cut-off but rather a step forward out of the liturgical dilemma. The Pope will soon set the old Mass alongside all the new forms again as the primordial measure of the liturgy—like the unalterably standardized platinum bar in Sèvres, France, for the metric system.

In the ruins of Byzantium—Ankara,
Ephesus, Istanbul, November 29, 2006

Turkey is a holy but also a difficult land, in which the visionary John foresaw and wrote down the Christian apocalypse almost two thousand years ago. The red shoes with which the Pope set foot on it on Tuesday are an inheritance from the Emperor of Byzantium. Those shoes were the only remaining way to identify the last Emperor of the Eastern Roman Empire on May 29, 1453, when he was found under mountains of fallen soldiers. It was the end of Eastern Rome. The conquest of the city by Sultan Mehmed at that time transformed Constantinople overnight into Istanbul. Since then "Europe" came into use also as the name for the former "Western Roman" Occident—to which Turkey too now mightily wants to belong, as Premier Erdogan once again emphasized after his tête-à-tête conversation at the airport. And now the Pope says that he will support him in this cause!

Father Lombardi, the Vatican press spokesman, could not confirm the statement. Moreover the separation of Church and State, as it has developed in a long process in the West, would forbid religions from having any direct political power or influence; the Pope himself explained once again that evening in the presence of diplomats that such activities and ambitions simply are "not the province of religion." The Vatican's official position has long been that Turkey must satisfy the criteria for entrance into the European Union. But one EU Commission after another determines that that very condition has still not been fulfilled. This is why no one was surprised that the first pictures of the foreign guest with his irritated hosts showed a rather awkward get-together—for example, someone to the right or the left of the Pope was constantly offering him a cup of mocha, or something else to drink or a biscuit, during his conversations in Ankara.

Istanbul today throbs like Manhattan. In recent decades it has exploded—and become the largest city on the European continent, even though the residents still do not seem to know exactly whether they now belong to the West or to the East, to Europe or to Asia. The only undisputed fact is that Turkey today belongs entirely and utterly to the House of Islam. This complete Islamization had not been achieved, however, during the 500-year rule of the Ottomans over the formerly Byzantine Empire, but paradoxically mainly through the radical process of secularization that Mustafa Kemal Ataturk decreed for the laicist Turkish state in one of the major acts of violence in the last century. It was a spectacular *"ordre du mufti"* [order from the mufti] with which the founder of the Turkish State tried to prop up the final result of that process that took the states of the West hundreds of years and an era of religious wars. Now, during the papal visit, it therefore seems as though the iron hand of the founder is evident against the impressive skyline of so many mosques in Istanbul, especially in the legions of policemen that encounter the visitor every fifty meters along the way. A lot was sacrificed to the Turkish nationalization process. Among the first victims were the Christians of Turkey, as a sort of strategic pawn sacrifice in return for the difficult moves that had been required of the large Muslim majority here for three generations. Now the Pope is visiting above all the pitiable remnant of ancient Turkish-Byzantine Christendom. Around eighty years ago Christians still made up some twenty percent of the population, but now just under 0.5 percent. It is a tiny minority that has grown too old and is dying out.

Only in the last century, therefore, has Turkey really become a land of Christian apocalypse; already in the first century the visionary John had frightened its flourishing communities with the prophecy: "I will remove your lampstand from its place." That came about long ago. Turkey is littered with ruins of precious basilicas of the early Christian period. Nowhere did Christendom grow so quickly at the beginning as here and in Egypt, and scarcely anywhere else was it so tragically uprooted and driven out too. The Pope is now trying again, with gentle irony, to address the multifaceted dilemma of this history with a quotation from the Middle Ages. It is older than the words of the Byzantine ruler Paleologos that became famous in Regensburg; this quotation is from the history of the Popes, by Gregory VII from the year 1076, and now he addresses it to Professor Ali Bardakoğlu, who a few weeks ago labeled him as having a "Crusader mentality." These are words, he begins, that his predecessor addressed "to a Muslim prince from North Africa.... Gregory VII spoke about the particular love that Christians and Muslims owe each other. For we believe in and witness to the one God, albeit in different ways; every day we praise Him and honor Him as the Creator of the centuries and the Lord of this world."

If Benedict XVI had had his way, he probably would have liked most to visit Antakya, ancient Antioch, where Christ's followers of both Jewish and pagan origin were called "Christians" for the first time in history. Security concerns, above all, prevented that. The regime has many misgivings about the activities of the Ecumenical Patriarch Bartholomew I, and every one of its moves entails heavy surveillance of all his actions. That is why he ended the second day of his journey with a visit to the Nightingale Hill behind Ephesus, to "Mary's House," one of the most beautiful and most mysterious places in Christendom, where he prayed the Hail Mary in Turkish: *"Aziz Meryem Mesih'in Annesi bizim için Dua et. Amen."* Above it the silver sky of the Aegean Sea. Flickering autumn foliage. Oaks and pines. Wild cyclamens surround the remote little house, as though on a Galilean hill in the Holy Land.

Ten kilometers [6 miles] away is the tomb of the Apostle John in Ephesus. A marble slab, four turned, free-standing pillars in the ruin of a basilica, a few lizards that scurry over the rubble, and that's it. Solitude. The tomb was empty, they say, when it was opened centuries ago. Only a handful of dust reportedly lay on the bottom of it, which the wind immediately carried off. A starker contrast with the basilicas over the tombs of the Princes of the Apostles Peter and Paul in Rome is scarcely imaginable.

The hours of the final unity — Istanbul, November 30, 2006

The voice of the muezzin reaches out in the dark for the hearts of those who are sleeping. Did it also wake the Pope? The wind blows recited prayers over the strait. Clouds drift over Istanbul. For days now it has looked like rain. After the autumnal gleam over Ephesus, the Bishop of Rome wakes up today in the summer residence of the Apostolic Nunciature, where the Nuncio Angelo Roncalli once lived — and as his successor on the papal throne he has remembered him again and again during these days. Because this "good Pope" "loved" the Turks so much. Because time is running short, especially in these days and hours too. The appointment book is very full for the seventy-nine-year-old man.

Benedict Up Close

Benedict XVI says Mass in the chapel with his secretary; then they set out over cordoned-off streets to the "Lighthouse," the Phanar. It is the spiritual goal of this strenuous journey: a run-down corner of the splendid metropolis on the Bosporus.

In contemporary Turkey, the traditional Greek district is the suspiciously eyed remnant of the capital of a sunken empire, even older than the sunken Ottoman Empire, older than Islam. This is why, along with the calls to prayer from the minarets on this Thursday, the feast day of the Apostle Andrew also began in this historical enclave. The Apostle himself founded this episcopal see of Byzantium; afterward Emperor Constantine I built the Second Rome on top of it, as the new capital of the East. John Chrysostom, Gregory of Nazianzen and "a host of witnesses" made the see venerable and renowned. Great names that hardly anyone in the West still recognizes—except the Pope, of course, to whom they are even more familiar than many contemporaries whom he meets with day after day.

The exact schedule of this trip is kept secret for security reasons. Probably no one told him about the gridlock that his visit caused in Istanbul and the many thousand curses in the omnipresent traffic jam. Nothing is running any more. The Galata Bridge is closed. Taxi drivers drive in a circle and finally leave their passengers off somewhere in despair. *"Taksi yok!"*—"No taxi!" But for hours now no unauthorized person has been able to get through to the Phanar by foot either. In Italy the lead story in the newspapers is Al Quaeda's threat to kill the Pope in Istanbul, because yesterday above Ephesus at Mary's House he dared to pray for peace for Jerusalem and for all peoples—of course as a pretext for a new Crusade whereby Turkey is to be carved out of the House of Islam again. Today will probably not go as smoothly and cheerfully as yesterday did in the silvery light of the Aegean on the Nightingale Hill. Helicopters plow through the sky with an ominous clatter. Not even President Bush experienced such tightly corseted security in Istanbul; but then again, he was not visiting an ancient sister metropolis of Washington.

The Armenian Patriarch is already waiting for the Pope, along with the Syrian Orthodox Metropolitan and the Chief Rabbi of Turkey. He will visit the Hagia Sophia, spend time in prayer in the Blue Mosque, but above all he will celebrate the "Divine Liturgy" today together with Patriarch Bartholomew I. It is the "centerpiece of the visit," as was previously announced by the Vatican: a new milestone in the reconciliation of feuding ancient Churches that began on December 7, 1965, when in Rome and in Constantinople the mutual excommunications were solemnly revoked. Ecumenism has progressed further with the Patriarch of Constantinople than with any other separated particular Church.

Milestone or not, the human liturgy rather than the divine built a few stumbling blocks into the celebration. The incense, the sputtering candles, the gold of the iconostas, the incessant singing of the choir, the hymn-laden liturgy of Saint John Chrysostom (whose remains lie on the cathedral premises)—every detail demonstrates once again to the guest from Rome in his ermine-lined scarlet mozetta [cape] the "splendid heritage of this place" where "the message of the Gospel and the cultural tradition of antiquity met."

Maybe it reminded him also of eternity and of how dependent the life of Christendom is on various traditions and therefore "breathes with two lungs," as his predecessor from Poland never tired of saying. The Pope prays the Christian profession of faith with the Patriarch, both in Greek. It is the common foundation and ground between East and West. Yet two steps away from the

Pope, cunning hands reserved a place of honor in the Divine Liturgy for Vuk Drašković too, the bearded Foreign Minister of Serbia, who has made a name for himself in the West as the author of the book *The Knife*. The fact that church and state are so difficult to separate in Islam—as the Turks nevertheless have almost recklessly tried to do for eighty years—is not least significantly a legacy from Byzantium.

"Your visit could not have come at a better time," the Lebanese diplomat in Ankara told the Pope two days earlier. "Peace is not merely the absence of war; nor can it be reduced solely to the maintenance of a balance of power between enemies," the Pontiff quoted a Conciliar document afterward in French. The developments of recent years, the phenomenon of terrorism and certain regional conflicts had only made clear once again the necessity of respect for the decisions of international institutions. Here he was thinking in particular about the "troubling conflict in the Near East, which shows no sign of abating and weighs heavily on the international community." Then in English he gently called for "religious freedom as the fundamental expression of human freedom in general," for Turkey also, which "has always served as a bridge between East and West and Asia and Europe, and as a turnstile of cultures and religions."

With the Patriarch, who remained in Istanbul as the last viceroy of a wrecked world empire (when Constantinople and its last Emperor had fallen), Benedict now draws quite different conclusions from history. Because "the process of secularization is persistently weakening Christian traditions," their common efforts can have no other goal than the "full communion of the Church of Rome with the Church of Constantinople." The divisions that exist among Christians are "a scandal to the world and an obstacle to the spread of the Gospel." The unity of Christians is vitally necessary for the freedom of the whole world. There can and must be frank discussion about all controversies.

After the liturgy both raise their arms high on the balcony of the inner courtyard, like two boxers after a victory—after a blessing in Latin and Greek. Both know: Constantinople would never have fallen if Christianity had been united. In vain had Emperor Constantine XI begged the Pope for help then. The latter refused; Byzantium would have to fulfill his conditions first. Deep down, November 30 today is therefore reminiscent also of May 28, 1453. "People from all sides streamed to the great Church of Holy Wisdom [i.e., *Hagia Sophia*]," it says in an old account of that last day, before the walls of Constantinople were breached. "Scarcely any citizens, except for the soldiers on the walls, stayed away from the desperate rogation service. Priests who viewed union with Rome as a mortal sin stepped up to the altar and celebrated the Divine Liturgy together with their brothers who were in favor of union. Everyone had come to make their confession and to receive Communion, regardless of whether the priest was an Orthodox or a Catholic. The golden mosaics with the images of Christ shimmered in the light of a thousand lamps and candles. Beneath them the priests moved for the last time in their magnificent vestments to the solemn rhythm of the liturgy. At that moment the Church was united."

Dialogue in Brazil, China, and Austria—and about the Old Rite of the Tridentine Mass—2007

Finger-wrestling in the Vatican—Rome, March 27, 2007
In the history of the Catholic world there is hardly a precedent to be found for the reinstatement of the old Latin rite of 1570 by Benedict XVI. This step will change the Church. The shy Pope almost single-handedly put this masterful change on the agenda, against enormous resistance. For this reason too, many never expected that he would not avoid this conflict but rather unswervingly seek to settle it according to his view—including many a cardinal who two years ago intended with Joseph Ratzinger to elect another transitional pope. And many coworkers and dignitaries of the Roman Curia were not counting on it at all. For instance, the catafalque on which the body of John Paul II lay in state in Saint Peter's Basilica from April 4 to 8, 2005, has still not been moved to the basement two years later. Instead the bier was just stowed away behind the organ in a side aisle near the tomb of Clement X. Beside it are stacks of plastic chairs with which the rows of seats in the Basilica can be replenished

quickly when too many guests come. A sheet of plastic covers
the cloth lining of the catafalque, as though it were just waiting behind the organ to be brought out again tomorrow, so as
to be able to offer the German Pope too a final resting place
on earth. The bier behind the organ, of course, is not waiting.
Nevertheless, what are those who left it hidden in this Baroque
junk-room waiting for?

The self-assured culture of Italian *"menefreghismo"* (a sort
of impassive indifference), along with many examples of leg-
endarily practical nonchalance, can perhaps best explain why
the forces of inertia that want nothing to be changed are so utterly and extraordinarily strong in the Vatican. For what could
possibly be more Italian than the Vatican? Former Secretary
of State Cardinal Sodano rather tenaciously refuses to vacate
his official residence. Tarcisio Bertone, to whom it belongs as
his successor in that post, has to put up with a makeshift office
day after day. On Sunday, at Evening Prayer at Saint Peter's,
once again three canons with lightning speed held "Veronica's
veil" up high in a silver frame from the gallery of the Veronica
Pillar, even though everyone in Rome knows by now that it
cannot possibly be displaying the ancient true image. It is too
big, it is not transparent, it in no way matches the old copies
of the *"vera ikon."* Dante would not have dedicated a single
verse of his *Divine Comedy* to that piece of cloth. What is the
meaning of all this? Little obvious facts only seldom have a
chance against very old traditions in the Eternal City. Such
procedures could be misinterpreted as a supreme disdain for
reality. Yet that is true only in a qualified sense. Conditions
are as they were in ancient Rome — one therefore hears as the
refrain of many complaints among foreigners — and of course
that is true in many respects.

For the strength of ancient Rome in fact lay also in its stubborn, sheer persistence. In this milieu, Joseph Ratzinger was already a foreign body, because he was always a preserver and a mover: a true conservative. Even more so now as Benedict XVI. The Pope from the land of Luther passionately opposes the leaden persistence that today, in Rome as in the rest of the Universal Church, is nevertheless often and paradoxically not conservative, but rather an insistence on the liberal spirit of the times of the last forty years. And so the power struggle between him and a big ideological faction in the Church has now come to a head, not in overdue personnel decisions, but rather in a passionate conflict over the old rite of the Tridentine Mass that had been banned by the reformers. Soon Benedict XVI will again allow free access to the venerable old liturgy that Pope Paul VI had abolished [*sic*] and replaced in 1969 with an unprecedented stroke of the pen—after it had developed for 2,000 years and even longer, because many parts of it were connected also with the liturgy of the Jewish Temple. In taking this step, Benedict XVI heeded the petitions of neither the French nor the German cardinals and bishops—and of course he was unimpressed by the various debates on European opinion pages. *Il Corriere della Sera* reported that he will authorize the use of the old Mass everywhere, without the approval and permission of the local bishop—which was usually granted with restrictions if at all—when at least thirty Catholics requested it. This is the masterful revision of a cultural revolution that the Pope has been conducting for two years now in office. If nothing happens to him—God forbid—his Decree (*Motu proprio*) on the liberation of the Tridentine liturgy is coming very soon, as certainly as the Amen in church. An accompanying letter to all the bishops has already been prepared. The matter has been decided. There will be no system reset, as one might imagine with a computer that has crashed. Benedict XVI is just giving back to the Catholic liturgy its primordial measure; from now on the new rite of 1969, which has become disoriented in many respects, can again be guided decisively by it. A surprisingly cosmic sort of finger-wrestling prepared the way for the decision. But after all, finger-wrestling is a Bavarian specialty.

Ad multos annos! Many years! —*Rome, April 12, 2007*

This Monday the gentle man from Marktl celebrates his eightieth birthday and enjoys the best of health. His monastic-Benedictine life style does not necessarily stand in the way of his doing that. In the midst of all the festivities of these days, surely he will have to grin somewhat unpapally about the fact that many in the Vatican and among the cardinals worldwide are still frightened by the nightmare scenario that the obstinate Pope from the North might live to be ninety-three years old like Leo XIII. He would probably respond to that concern today merely by remarking, "Well, we do not want to set limits on God's goodness," with a malicious deeper meaning. This, nevertheless, is the man who two years ago saw his election to the papacy coming at him at first like a "guillotine blade" in the conclave. His pious sarcasm is legendary, yet in one respect the image of the guillotine was correct. In a twinkling of the eye the decision separated his new life from his old one. The worldwide public, though, was able to learn only afterward who this man is. For the election also separated his public perception with a single cut from the boogeyman that a few media specialists had cobbled together and tirelessly publicized: the *Panzerkardinal* from Nazi Germany. That media filter shattered on April 19, 2005, like the security glass of a windshield hit by a piece of gravel.

From then on, cameras too many to count in an uninterrupted series have zoomed in on Joseph Ratzinger for close-ups on the video screen. From that day on, countless women (and men) worldwide have fallen in love with the shy smile of the Pope from Germany, who had always charmed Roman women and men with his *"bella figura"* [fine appearance]. Since that day, Saint Peter's Square beneath the window of his Apostolic Palace has been filled Sunday after Sunday and one Wednesday after another, in a way that happened with John Paul II only on special feast days. The Germans especially—from the various denominations—are the ones who have tirelessly streamed into Saint Peter's Square as pilgrims. For two years Germany has acquired a new center of gravity in Rome—or rightfully rediscovered it, as the first Pope from the land of the Reformation would probably put it.

Interest in the Pope and the papacy has experienced an enormous boom during this time. Amazon Books automatically lists 1,222 hits today when you type the word "Pope" into its search engine, many of them with extremely ludicrous titles. To date, in any case, it is far from certain whether all these phenomena signal a turning point or have only opened a temporary window that could close again just as quickly after Benedict XVI. The Pope, nevertheless, persistently does everything he can to make sure that that does not happen. He had intended to write the first volume of his book about Jesus of Nazareth during the days of his retirement; instead he has eked it out, page by page, from "all the free moments" of his life as the Successor of Peter. A short summary of the contents? At the end of the modern era the Pope again raises the question of God in the Western world and answers it abruptly with unambiguous clarity that has not been heard in a long time: "Jesus Christ is none other than the

Son of the living God." Even before its appearance, the difficult book topped best-seller lists worldwide. He is one of the most respectable ambassadors that secular or even Protestant Germany ever had.

In two years Benedict XVI has already made history. As an old man, without spectacular gestures, usually quietly and often in surprising ways. In Cologne he presided in August 2005 over the largest religious gathering since the end of the War. In Regensburg the Pope, with the demeanor of an ivory-tower professor, gave one of the most moving speeches of the new century—and just weeks later won the hearts of the Muslims with a quiet prayer in Istanbul's Blue Mosque. With every step he takes, moreover, the master thinker is still learning—and he still learns quickly. One may doubt, nevertheless, whether he will ever grasp the laws of the media world as his predecessor did. He does know, though, that the media show is anything but a true mirror of reality.

His knowledge of human nature is not on a par with his predecessor's either; he is too wise to be unaware of that. That is why he is not focusing his waning strength on overdue personnel decisions, but rather on his effort to restore the space of the sacred in the world, the breakdown of which over the last fifty years he experienced like a collapsing cathedral. In order to build up this space again, he will soon allow the old 1570 Latin ritual again, with a signature in tiny handwriting: *Benedictus XVI*.

It is I—Rome, April 13, 2007

The Mount of the Beatitudes in Galilee is "the new Sinai" of Christendom. "Anyone who has been there," Joseph Ratzinger writes in Chapter Four of his new book, *Jesus of Nazareth*, the last chapters of which he completed as Pope Benedict XVI, "and gazed with the eyes of his soul on the wide prospect of the waters of the lake, the sky and the sun, the trees and the meadows, the flowers and the sound of birdsong can never forget the wonderful atmosphere of peace and the beauty of creation encountered there—in a land unfortunately so lacking in peace." The Sinai experience of Elijah "is completed here": as one of the prophets of Israel he had already experienced God's closeness and the passing by of the Almighty, not in the storm or in the earthquake or in the fire, but in the still, small breeze.

The Pope's book is perhaps most moving where his analysis of the four Gospels is reflected in this way in the "fifth Gospel," as the Holy Land has often been called. With the extraordinary exertion that any book demands of an eighty-year-old author, nevertheless, Benedict XVI intends not only to move his readers but also to enlighten them. For major parts of the roughly four hundred pages the great systematic theologian therefore does not sit together with Jesus of Nazareth on the new Sinai or some other hill in Galilee, nor as Professor Pope who finally could proclaim new dogmas from the Chair of Peter, but rather as a master thinker in the "grove of Academe," where he argues and debates with the scribes of the past century about the appropriate interpretation of the Gospels "from the Baptism in the Jordan to the Transfiguration."

So for long stretches the book becomes dense and laborious rather than beautiful and moving, being a highly complex masterpiece, inevitably with sentences like this one [p. 333]: "Volker Hampel holds that Jesus' words about the 'ransom for many' are derived not from Isaiah 53:10-12, but from Proverbs 21:18 and Isaiah 43:3 ... [which] strikes me as very unlikely." In any case the volume has many different levels in different styles, in a sort of theological collection of short stories about the Sermon on the Mount, the Our Father and the major parables. Yet long stretches consist of a debate with Rudolf Schnackenburg, Joachim Jeremias, Adolf von Harnack, Hartmut Gese, Oscar Cullmann, Harald Riesenfeld, Adolf Jülicher—and of course with the Church Fathers from Augustine to Gregory of Nyssa. He is grappling here with the wide spectrum of modern theology, and the surprising thing about it is not the many Protestant names but rather how decisively the Christian world has been stamped by the Germans since the days of Luther.

In these not always hallowed halls, Benedict/Ratzinger confronts them here as one of the most prominent Germans to date from the land of the Reformation, endowed with a phenomenal memory, well-versed like few others with the writings of Dante or the thinkers of the Enlightenment; with gentle sarcasm he makes fun of exegetes whose learned essays have to be seen "as more akin to a 'Jesus novel' than as an actual interpretation of the texts." He twists debates in which one gets lost as though in a "graveyard of mutually contradictory hypotheses" or where much of the logic "might be appropriate for rigorous professorial thinking [but] it does not suit the complexity of living reality." By all means that must be meant here and there as a self-criticism also. "It is not the Scripture experts, those who are professionally concerned with God, who recognize (Jesus of Nazareth); they are too caught up in the intricacies of their detailed knowledge." Whether with his insights he could ever qualify today as a lecturer on any theological faculty in Germany is highly questionable.

There is no doubt, however, that this is no longer an *Introduction to Christianity*, with which the genial theologian made a stir in his younger years; this book is very deliberately designed for the later and most advanced curriculum. What may first grab the attention of the lay reader, therefore, is the remark that the head of the Catholic Church makes about the great Jewish scholar Jacob Neusner: "More than other interpretations known to me, this respectful and frank dispute between a believing Jew and Jesus, the son of Abraham, has opened my eyes to the greatness of Jesus' words and to the choice that the gospel places before us." But Joseph Ratzinger always tried to decipher the Gospels from the perspective of the Jewish texts of the Torah, "in the world in which Jesus was at home, and the Judaism in which Jesus lived"—and to interpret Jesus of Nazareth in an overarching canonical exegesis that includes all the texts of both the Old and the New Testament at once. Thus the book automatically, as it were, became a revision also of many experiments in which the image of Jesus in recent decades crumbled away in many respects like a deteriorating fresco. What in many schools of thought appears to be nothing more than isolated pieces of a puzzle, Joseph "Benedict" Ratzinger tries here with his last strength to put back together again like an ancient, broken but precious icon.

To see Jesus Christ as man and God at the same time is actually a self-evident, fundamental article of the Christian Creed. Formulating it in a new way, nevertheless, is considered a sensation today, even though nothing else was to be expected of Joseph Ratzinger, who as Pope took the name of Saint Benedict also on account of his central admonition "to prefer nothing to the love of Christ." The theologian Thomas Söding from Wuppertal says that "in Jesus scholarship after the Enlightenment nothing more was said" about Jesus as the true Son of God. Never before in history was there a Pope who wrote a scholarly book on Jesus. This shows a brand new style of papacy, in which the Vicar of Christ on earth does not formulate dogma but presents his observations as a theologian for discussion. That is revolutionary. The Pope dared to go "into the trenches of the exegetes," as Klaus Berger in Heidelberg marvels.

This book is not easy reading; it matter-of-factly uses technical terms like "eschaton" or the "kenosis" of Jesus, and a large part of is dedicated to a debate with exegetes whom, outside of graduate seminars, no one has heard of in Germany, much less in Africa, America, Asia or Australia. Probably many people expected something else from the new Supreme Pastor of the Universal Church. Nevertheless, it is hardly surprising that the difficult volume has already taken the best-seller lists by storm, even before its publication, with a first printing of 150,000 copies in Germany alone and translations into more than thirty languages. It is a "popular direct hit," the "Lutheran journalist" Peter Hahne claims to have observed in advance. Whether this debate with theologians of all faith traditions is also the major ecumenical pitch of the first pope from the land of the Reformation that many expect of him, only the future will show. Their answer will prove the extent to which they are willing to respond to the challenges which culminate in the Pope's remarks: "The cross of Jesus is the burning bush," Jesus of Nazareth is "the Holy Tabernacle," He is "the Sabbath." Indeed, He is "the Torah" itself. "He comes from God; He is God." This is not only the central thesis of this book. Provocatively, the Pope is trying here as a scholar to demonstrate that Jesus saw it in exactly this way. All the words of the Bible "waited, so to speak" for Him—for "Christ, the Son of the living God."

With the enormous response to this difficult masterpiece, might something of that initial "fear of God" be breaking into the Western world again? Something of the fear that shows not simply the "familiar Jesus" but rather the presence of God

Himself, as experienced by the Apostles "who were completely beside themselves" as they saw the "I AM WHO AM" in the flesh walking toward them across the storm-tossed waters of the Sea of Galilee, and He called to them: "Take courage! It is I. Do not fear!"

Writing this book is the fulfillment of an old, lifelong dream of Joseph Ratzinger, for which he had already reserved the final years of his life. Now everything has turned out quite differently, and he used all his free time as Pope to write it down—while quite a few in the corridors of the Vatican asked in whispers whether the Pontifex Maximus didn't have more important and better things to do than to write books. As of today this question has been answered. He had nothing more important to do. It is the expression of his "personal search 'for the Face of the Lord,'" he says in the Foreword. He welcomes contradicting views; he asks the "readers for that initial goodwill without which there can be no understanding." Will the readers recognize the "Face of the Lord" better after reading this book? Does Jesus of Nazareth come to meet them in this book, flesh and blood, as he came to doubting Thomas on the Sunday after Easter? Surely this search is not yet at its destination. After Volume I we are still waiting for Volume II of this theological "biography" of Jesus—on His childhood, His Passion, and the altogether decisive Resurrection. So the eighty-year-old man in Rome still has the most difficult and most important part to do.

Outstretched arms—Rio de Janeiro, May 12, 2007

Benedict XVI had no trouble winning the understanding of Brazilian men and women. More quickly than was expected in Rome, Paris, or Berlin, the man who is probably the last European on the papal throne won their hearts too. He embodies "the quintessence of European Catholicism," wrote *The New York Times* before the journey. In Brazil he would "not have much to say." For the biggest Catholic nation had turned into a jumbled "religious mosaic" in which numerous Pentecostals have long since been making inroads among the people more efficiently than the Catholic priests. In short: The Pontiff would not be able to win back the country. Even Cláudio Cardinal Hummes, the former Archbishop of São Paulo, feared that Latin America could "be lost." That is why the Pope came. The loss of Latin America would do "enormous and irreparable harm to the Catholic Church." Hummes is not just anybody. In the last conclave he was still considered, along with Joseph Ratzinger, a favorite candidate to succeed John Paul II, to whom hearts here had always flown like swallows.

Many observers and so-called papal experts were all the more surprised, suddenly to discover a downright dancing lightness of step in the old lemonade drinker from Marktl am Inn during his visit to the samba nation. Three thousand two hundred journalists, instead of the expected two thousand, accompanied the event, and now they had to report back to their native countries in bewilderment the impression that the eighty-year-old Pope made on this journey: flexible, charming and sure-footed as a sleepwalker. After the grueling flight from Rome, he got off the airplane manifestly younger and better-rested than all who accompanied him. He made this impression afterward, too, at all the altars where he celebrated great solemn Masses and gave the Brazilians a good talking-to in a friendly way. Millions lined the streets through which he passed in São Paulo and poured into the Pacaembu Stadium or onto Campo de Marte [Mars Field]: the favorite arenas of Brazilian sports and music fans, whether they came now from the famous infamous *"favelas"* [slums] without running water at the edge of the city or from the heavily guarded villas in the districts on the hills. Nowhere did Benedict XVI give them a discount, quite unlike the new sects: Adventists, Dollarists, voodoo cults or other instant religions from the far North, which south of the Rio Grande are fond of allowing and forgiving everything that actually should be forbidden, in return for cash in advance.

Is this now therefore already a Catholic re-conquest of the pearl of this "continent of hope" (John Paul II), where unfortunately despair all too often peeks out from around the nearest corner, in horrible poverty, violence, and demoralization? Certainly not. Yet not only the future can hold surprises but the present too. The string tanga was invented on the Catholic Copacabana beach, before conquering Europe as well and the rest of the world later. Now the world may be most astonished at how the Pope on this trip, to the enormous applause of the Brazilians, defends "the sanctity of marriage and premarital chastity" against all attacks—and as he does so stretches out his arms in blessing over the young people of this country as wide as the Christ figure over the Sugarloaf Mountain of Rio de Janeiro.

Salt of the Earth—Rome, Beijing, July 1, 2007

On Pentecost Sunday, Benedict XVI signed a forty-eight-page letter. The original language of the document is Chinese. It is an exceedingly kind and courteous letter which the Pope addresses to the bishops, priests, consecrated religious, and lay faithful of the Catholic Church in the People's Republic of China—and for that reason alone, it is tremendously explosive. The "little flock" of China to which the successor of Peter in Rome writes includes roughly thirteen million members and is the fastest, most dynamically growing part of the Catholic world—in which, as he puts it, the "Church universal" is also ever-present in the midst of the Middle Kingdom. Unmistakably present at the same time is also his express claim that the unity of the Church is grounded in the office of the pope. Moreover, his ministry as successor of the Apostle Peter belongs "intrinsically to the essence of every particular Church." For precisely this claim, untold numbers of people have endured untold suffering in China over the last sixty years. For all the friendliness of its tone, the Pope makes no secret of it—again in order to reset talks with the Communist government of the People's Republic.

"Fear not, little flock," he writes both to those Catholics of China loyal to Rome and to those in bondage to Peking. "You are the salt of the earth, you are the light of the world." Reuniting the Church, which was divided in 1951 by Mao Zedong, is explicitly one of the main purposes of this initiative. "In the Church, no one is a stranger," he continues a bit farther on, in order nevertheless to exhort the "shepherds and the faithful" unmistakably to protect and defend courageously the doctrine and tradition of the Catholic Church from all attacks and any sort of coercion; he also calls upon the state, whose attitude toward all religions is still characterized by despotism and uncertainty after an era of great repression, to respect full religious freedom.

A similar conflict has perhaps not existed since the days of Gregory VII and Henry IV during the High Middle Ages. Benedict XVI, with his letter, intends to defuse it. Unlike Henry IV, however, the powers that be in China these days are not Christian rulers. With this conciliatory manifesto, the Pope nevertheless moves to engage them today in a way the government in

Peking has never experienced. "In view of the challenges faced by the Chinese people," the document, however, is also an extraordinary offer of dialogue and of the Vatican's assistance at many levels in the difficult process of globalization. The Church cannot and may not be "identified with any political community, nor is it bound to any system." To this end, Benedict XVI cites the Chinese missionary Matteo Ricci (1552-1610), who had assured the Emperor of China in his time that the Catholic Church asked for "no privileges whatever from China and its leaders," and instead only "the resumption of dialogue, based on mutual respect and ever deeper understanding." The Emperor of China and his advisers were skeptical even then, for the duration of a narrow window of opportunity. It will be no different today with China's political class in the Communist Party. The Vatican has no right to interfere in China's internal affairs, an initial statement by the government said—while the Pope's letter was still hushed up in China's churches on Sunday.

Nevertheless, the document can already be regarded as a new milestone in a long, shared history whose often brutal dislocations the Pope repeatedly describes politely as "misunderstandings." What effect the letter will have among China's divided Catholics is uncertain. The same can be said of the reaction to this initiative by Beijing's suspicious leaders. Every page of the carefully composed document will irritate many. It begins with the prophetic analysis in which the Pope from Germany cites the Pope from Poland: Asia's bishops wrote twelve years ago that in the first Christian millennium the Cross was planted in Europe, in the second millennium in America and Africa, and that "now in the third millennium, a great harvest of faith in the immense expanse of the pulsating Asian continent" awaits Christianity.

Recapturing sacred space (in the secular world) —
Rome, July 8, 2007

The decision of Pope Benedict XVI to restore full and natural rights in the Catholic Church to the Tridentine liturgy as of September 14 is perhaps best illustrated by a small example. Every Sunday at 5:00 p.m., the old Gregorian Vespers are begun in the choir of St. Peter's Basilica with the words of Psalm 70: "*Deus, in adiutorium meum intende. / Domine ad adiuvandum me festina*" (O God, come to my assistance. / Lord, make haste to help me). It is a moving hour. Only a short time ago, during this same hour, the feet of thousands of tourists in the basilica shuffled at the same time behind the choir to marvel at art treasures, to take pictures or to telephone their loved ones. For this house of God is also a matchless treasure chest, attracting visitors from all over the world like a magnet. However, when Benedict XVI appointed Archbishop Angelo Comastri archpriest of the Basilica last October, it was one of his first measures to allow visitors, during vespers, to approach only as far as the Bernini altar, almost a hundred yards from those praying in the choir. Since then massive wooden barriers and attentive guards have stopped all guests who do not wish to take part in the Gregorian liturgy. The order can also be understood symbolically: as an expansion and recapturing of sacred space within the Church that is besieged by secularization.

For most people, St. Peter's Basilica has long since become a museum, in which the Church cannot withhold her art treasures from the world. It is the same space in which the Second Vatican Council met from 1962 to 1965. Here moved the oft-invoked spirit of "*aggiornamento*" (the "updating" of the Catholic Church), a term that "good Pope John" XXIII coined. Yet, during the Council and after it, the old Tridentine liturgy was of course still celebrated according the 1962 Missal, and was even a "power source" for all the Council Fathers, as Bishop Hanke from Eichstatt says today. The fact that the Pope has once again generally allowed this liturgy cannot be viewed in quite the same way as the minor technical move by the Archpriest of St. Peter's, yet it breathes the same spirit. It is not a matter of calling into question the Council or even the new liturgy since the reform in 1970. But the step is an attempt to recapture the sacred: an expansion of the mysterious inner space of the Church, which must be guarded from the incursions of banalization. "One can be at home only where mystery dwells," said the great theologian of the Council, Karl Rahner. The statistics are clear: in recent decades many have become homeless in the Catholic Church. How it came to that, despite all good intentions, will perhaps remain a mystery.

Pope Paul VI, who had ushered in the radical change of the liturgy in 1969, admitted on June 29, 1972, his sense that "the smoke of Satan has entered the temple of God through some fissure." The puzzling "smoke" was, however, perhaps only an overdose of the spirit of the age to which the Church had then opened itself up. It was a spirit that had many names. Among students, it produced communes and other utopias, in the Third World—totalitarian Communist movements, and in the Church, in those days, "*communio*" became the magic word: community! For this reason, the priest had to turn about-face, in order to gather together with the congregation around the altar, like scouts around a camp fire. For this reason, Latin was ditched, for this reason, new songs were composed and the sign of peace was introduced. There was much good in it, and even more goodwill, but also a spirit that was never quite free of ideological blindness and arbitrariness. At the time, Cardinal Ottaviani, Cardinal Ratzinger's predecessor in the Holy Office, had already lamented it. That was why the baker's son from Trastevere, who was as round-headed as old Cato, became by acclamation the bogeyman of the Church in the days of the Council. True community, he maintained undauntedly, must first be grounded in communion with God. He saw that expressed conspicuously in the old liturgy, in the shared orientation toward the altar, in the countless saints for whom the ancient Mass had served as a home, in a mystery which had again and again become the source of many conversions. Ottaviani, at the time, remarked sarcastically about "*communio*" and collegiality of the bishops, that communal action of the Apostles is mentioned only once in the Bible, where it says, "And they all fled!" That was perhaps unfair. But now the Pope gives him too a fairer hearing—amidst a Zeitgeist which he now quite independently is confronting with new room for the worthy celebration of *all* divine worship.

Second home coming—Vienna, September 6, 2007

The temperature fell dramatically when the Pope landed on Austrian soil. Benedict XVI has a cold. Last week in Rome it was 109 degrees Fahrenheit; now it is 39 degrees Fahrenheit in Mariazell, the destination of his pilgrimage. Every morning in his private chapel in Rome the Pope looks at the gentle smile of the Madonna of Mariazell, which John Paul II brought from Austria to the Vatican years ago. As a child Joseph Ratzinger was able to see almost as far as Salzburg on clear days, from the castle heights above Tittmoning, where his father had been transferred as a local policeman. In those days, the city of Mozart was the nearest diocesan city.

"I have loved this land," he wrote to the Austrians before his arrival, "since the long Sunday walks which we took with our mother in the early 1930's, over the Salzach bridge to Ostermiething, to Sankt Radegund and to other localities on the Austrian side of the Salzach." Several of his ancestors came from Austria; his mother came from the South Tyrol. Not only Bavaria formed the background and origins of the Pope from Germany, but also the vast, wide world of the Hapsburgs. In a certain sense, this trip is therefore the second homecoming of his pontificate, which supplements and completes his spectacular first journey to Munich, Freising, Altötting and Regensburg two years ago. The Mariensäule, a tall monument to the Blessed Virgin, and the Judenplatz [Jewish Square] in Vienna are therefore among the first stops.

That decision, however, was not made during his pontificate, but already in 2004, when the Prefect of the Congregation for the Doctrine of the Faith first traveled to Mariazell and spontaneously agreed to return for the 850th anniversary celebrations in 2007. Now Pope, he did not want to go back on his word, given while still a cardinal — even though entirely different themes were to dominate the journey. For this time, the Pontiff is also visiting the "heart of Europe, which has given our faith so manifold and luminous a form that touches even people who do not have or no longer share the Christian faith, and yet love the beauty it has produced." While the Third European Ecumenical Gathering is taking place at the same time in Romanian Sibiu, he travels to Krakow and Auschwitz on his second pastoral visit in that old Central Europe where he will pay homage to the "*Magna Mater Austriae*" in Mariazell as well as to the "*Regina Hungarorum et Slavorum*," the "Great Mother of Austria" and "Queen of the Hungarians and Slavs."

But of course one cannot stop at such acts of homage, and perhaps the plunging temperature is the first signal for that. For in "that great culture which has grown over the centuries," today he wishes to engage above all "the wrestling and questioning of an ever more rapidly moving period," the "hardships of believing and of being a Christian while coexisting with different cultures and traditions." So, for instance, a confident defense of Sunday against the encroachment of secular modernity is but one theme among many in this package. "Look to Christ!" is the motto of the journey. It is a deeply Benedictine appeal. "Show us your ever youthful face" wrote the Pope on the same day a year ago to the Capuchins of Manoppello on the occasion of his visit to the "Holy Face." "Show us the human Face of God who has entered into history." What does that mean today? A veritable whirlpool of problems threatens to drag Austria into the deep. This homecoming is not exactly a home game.

Doctor Benedict — Mariazell, Vienna — September 7-9, 2007

At the destination of the papal pilgrim's journey stood the assembled bishops of the Church of Austria in the pouring rain. Did that signify something? Or was it simply jinxed? The festive vestments of the shepherds, specially crafted for the feast of the Nativity of Mary, looked as if they were yet again meant to illustrate the liturgical aberrations that especially afflict the Church of Austria. "Whenever in our thinking we are only concerned about making the liturgy attractive, interesting and beautiful, the battle is already lost," the Pope says a day later at Holy Cross Abbey [Heiligenkreuz]. At least with the design of these vestments at Mariazell the idea seems to have been as though someone — perhaps even a pious nun — wanted to express herself in the daring blue-yellow batik patterns; just like the architects who designed the altar platform with such a skimpy roof that it offered almost no protection against the rain. What a horror it must have been in the eyes of the Pontiff who has such a keen liturgical sense! But the view of the pious crowd in raincoats must have more than made up for it. While descending the steps of the altar platform after Mass, he slips on the soaking wet ground, stumbles briefly, but does not fall.

Regardless, the music was as good as it gets, at every stop on his journey. Where in Europe is music played more beautifully or more artfully sung? Just when the weather in the mountains finally gets downright miserable, Benedict XVI's voice warmed up and recovered almost completely in this land where every corner seems fully developed by the tradition of old Europe. The three-towered basilica in Mariazell is a gothic treasure house and a baroque bank vault. At Mass, the Pope celebrates the Sacrifice with the venerable Tessilo chalice of Kremsmunster Abbey, which weighs six pounds and is over 1,300 years old. In front of him, somewhere in the crowd, sits Otto von Habsburg with his family, not under plastic like all the others, but under his old floppy hat. *Noblesse oblige.*

The sheets of water falling from the sky, however, seem to be an image of the flood of secularism against which the Pope intended once again here to raise a levee around the Church so that She would not be washed away from this old "kingdom of monasteries," ["*Klöster-reich,*" a traditional pun on Österreich] in the heart of the Occident. He tries to do this with every word of his many multi-layered—and perhaps often too-many-layered—speeches during these days.

It does not take long. He has already arrived at the central themes of his pontificate. And Austria is very much opposed to him. The celebration of Sunday Mass in Saint Stephen's Cathedral is a celebration of perfect beauty. The old bell of the cathedral, the "Pummerin," thrums as he enters. The Missa Cellensis, the "Mariazell Mass" in Latin by Joseph Haydn, and Gregorian chant frame the mystery of the hour." "[The] attitude of resignation with regard to truth ... lies at the heart of the crisis of the West," he said yesterday. Today he says, "our light, our truth, our goal, our fulfillment, ... all this is not a religious doctrine but a person: Jesus Christ." Christians encounter him and the "wide open eyes of the crucified and risen Son of God" in the "gift of the Lord's day."

"Sine dominico non possumus!" He therefore repeats in Vienna a remark from his sermon in Bari last year. For he cannot defend Sunday any better than in the words of the Christians of North African Abitinia in the year 304, whom he quotes: "We cannot live without Sunday!" The first day of the week has been changed "in our Western societies into the week-end, into leisure time." This free time, however, should not be "wasted time." Sunday has liberated Christians from the toil and slavery of undifferentiated time. "We are heirs. The inheritance is love."

There is no question that the Pope loves Austria, where the crisis of the Church is so striking, because there is hardly another country of Europe that has been so richly endowed by the Church. Here we find the most significant remains of the Holy Roman Empire, whose peoples for a thousand years tried to journey as pilgrims toward the "heavenly Jerusalem." They thereby advanced Europe's history substantially. Austria too, however, has arrived at a post-Christian modernity, in which many forces try to push the Church into irrelevance. Austria's Church seems to have become "a little flock" with a great past. Some of the feverish reactions among Austrian Catholics can be explained by this enormous revolution. For that reason in Vienna, Mariazell, and Heiligenkreuz, the Pope sometimes looked less like a pilgrim than like a doctor laying his hand on the patient's forehead. At the end of his journey he had already lowered the patient's temperature a little by his warmth alone. Just then the skies opened over Vienna again—this time for the sun.

Spe salvi—*Saved in hope*—*Rome, November 30, 2007*

"The writings of the master gave no indication as to how to proceed," remarks Benedict XVI at one point in his new Encyclical. Yet he is not speaking here about Jesus of Nazareth, but Karl Marx. And neither is it exactly a pious remark. It is sheer sarcasm, which Joseph Ratzinger cannot resist while considering Lenin's perplexity after the successful October Revolution. The refined mockery from the pen of the Successor of Peter could just as well have come from the lips of a Voltaire. But the Pope is not a cynic. His document therefore did not become a triumphalist settling of scores with an era in which so many systems of thought have come crashing down like the Twin Towers in Manhattan—only with a far higher death toll. But he does analyze—laconically rather than melancholically—the process in which Christendom let themselves be deprived of the hope that Christians—and no one else—had once ushered into the world: a continuous reaching out to the future. They owed their present strength to this "looking ahead."

But the manifesto against the nihilism of an allegedly infinite emptiness behind all being, which Benedict XVI here develops again, is by no means a lampoon. "In the last two hundred years there have been too few who have tried to halt the seemingly inevitable turn of the wheel of modernity. But as everyone knows, hope grows in hardship," Alexander Gauland wrote just a few days ago. *Et voilà!* Hope is making a comeback here, as the most well-founded consolation. *"Spe salvi facti sumus"* are the first words of the second Encyclical of Benedict XVI, taken from the Letter of Paul to the Romans: "In hope we were saved!" This means that Christian faith does not provide an instant inner peace, but a goal that is worth every effort along the way: "The encounter with the God who in Christ has shown us His Face."

"It is not the elemental spirits of the universe, the laws of matter, which ultimately govern the world and mankind, but a personal God governs the stars, that is, the universe; it is not the laws of matter and of evolution that have the final say, but reason, will, love—a Person." Jesus was not a social revolutionary like Spartacus, nor a freedom fighter and false messiah like Bar Kochba, but rather he took "the encounter with the living God" into the world, with firm hope of meeting again. But if the encounter with this person is merely "informative" and not "performative," the Pope assures us, then it has not taken place at all. Then faith is only asserted and empty.

Christian hope transforms life, long before its fulfillment. Such faith is "not merely a personal reaching out towards things to come.... [It] draws the future into the present. The fact that this future exists changes the present."

Of course, the Encyclical must therefore also speak anew about eternity and eternal life—about the ultimate questions that appear to many theologians to be long since contaminated. The loftiness of the argument—and many a tangled, unedited Ratzingerian sentence—now and then launch the writing into satellite orbit. Back on the ground, however, with laser-controlled accuracy it hits the bull's eye of many contemporary debates—especially in Europe, where the unreasonable demands of so-called euthanasia are only one segment in a variety show of existential disputes. When he touches on the "moralism" of atheists since the eighteenth century, his intention is not merely to expose the insolence of Robespierre or the Reign of Terror by his Committee of Public Safety as a grisly aberration, but rather to hail it (for those who read between the lines) as a simple logical consequence. In the end, Communists confiscated Christian hope, in a last great Christian heresy. To this analysis Benedict XVI adds self-critically, that "we must also acknowledge that modern Christianity has limited the horizon of its hope and has failed to recognize sufficiently the greatness of its task."

Therefore, as spectacular as the Pope's critique of philosophers such as Engels, Horkheimer, or Adorno may seem to the rest of the world, the Encyclical often becomes densest in passages where he gazes in wonderment through his window at the stars of night, pondering thoughts like those of the young Isaac Bashevis Singer: "On the one hand, we do not want to die; above all, those who love us do not want us to die. Yet on the other hand, neither do we want to continue living indefinitely, nor was the earth created with that in view. So what do we really want?" To live forever? With Augustine, he continues to question in a dialogue across the millennia: "What in fact is 'life'? And what does 'eternity' really mean? There are moments when it suddenly seems clear to us: yes, this is what true 'life' is—this is what it should be like. Besides, what we call 'life' in our everyday language is not real 'life' at all." Instead, what we really want is only "the life which is simply life, simply 'happiness'. In the final analysis, there is nothing else that we ask for in prayer. Our journey has no other goal—it is about this alone."

For only someone who is touched by love begins to glimpse what "life" really is. The sheer "pursuit of happiness" guaranteed by the American Constitution is light years away from this sort of hope. From the temporality in which we are imprisoned, it is necessary to infer that "eternity is not an unending succession of days in the calendar, but something more like the supreme moment of satisfaction, in which totality embraces us and we embrace totality—this we can only attempt. It would be like plunging into the ocean of infinite love, a moment in which time—the before and after—no longer exists.... We must think along these lines if we want to understand the object of Christian hope...: our being with Christ."

November 30, the day on which the Pope presented the encyclical, is the feast day of the Apostle Andrew. The brother of Peter is considered the arch-patriarch of Orthodox Christianity. The date of the publication therefore underscores yet again the apostolic and ecumenical authority with which Benedict XVI presents this letter. Last year on Saint Andrew's Day, he had agreed with Bartholomew I in Istanbul on the "perfect communion of the Church of Rome with the Church of Constantinople." This year, on the same day as the Encyclical's publication, he had Cardinal Bertone, the Secretary of State, respond officially to the letter written to him by 138 Muslim leaders on October 13, as an invitation to a world premiere: to a dialogue with Islam deserving of the name. Therefore less importance should not be ascribed to either of the new Encyclicals. Before the Western world, the Pope outlines here the "crisis of ecclesiastical hope" along with his answer to it—from the roots that are common to all Christians. The fact that he does not mention the name Ernst Bloch and his *The Principle of Hope* should not surprise anyone. More surprising, though, is the fact that he defends the images of Christendom against Adorno, from the image of the Crucified to the image of the Last Judgment, which is "not primarily an image of terror, but an image of hope," perhaps even "the decisive image of hope." Hope for a final balance also completely pulls the rug out from under the theodicy controversy. This is the dispute over the question of how God could allow all the evil that we have come to know. "Where was God in Auschwitz?" "On the cross," says Robert Spaemann, the old friend of Joseph Ratzinger. But Benedict XVI now writes three times in a single letter about the fact that God has shown His Face in Christ. In the third year of his pontificate, the longing for a reunion with this countenance has become the polestar of his theology, but above all of his love, his faith—and his hope.

An Anticipated, Initial Afterword: From Ground Zero in Manhattan to the Grotto of Massabielle at the Foot of the Pyrenees — 2008

Seven years later, and more than a year since Benedict XVI had announced his resignation on February 11, 2013, I mailed him the following letter on June 29, 2014, addressed to the house "Mater Ecclesiae," his final home in the Vatican Gardens:

> Holy Father, for [the publishing house] Herbig Verlag in Munich I am compiling a collection of my articles in which I followed your pontificate from the first day to the last as a correspondent for the Berlin daily newspaper *Die Welt*. But now there is a slight problem. On March 6, 2008, I suffered a stroke, which put me out of commission for a year. For this year 2008 therefore I have not one single article about your pontificate in my files. May I ask you please to forward to me maybe three to five statements of any kind that you wrote that you consider especially important during that period of time? I would like to include these texts then in this book in a supplementary chapter. I would be very glad if you could do that. With cordial thanks and every good wish, P.B.

Benedict Up Close

About two weeks later, on Tuesday, July 15, our doorman gave me a package stamped URGENTE—A MANO (hand delivery) from the "*Segretaria di Stato*," the Vatican Secretariat of State. Inside the brown wrapping paper there was a high-class, sturdy, white two-part telescope container box. It weighed several kilos. Too heavy for our kitchen scale. On it the coat of arms of Benedict XVI printed in gold, with Augustine's shell, the bear of Friesing and the Moor beneath the miter. The whole thing was wrapped three times around with a centimeter-wide golden ribbon. It was a masterpiece of the art of packaging and probably the handiwork of Sister Birgit, as it seemed, the former secretary of the Pope emeritus.

In the carton there were two heavy books with the title *Insegnamenti di Benedetto XVI.*—IV, 1 (2008) and 2 (2008) (*Teachings of Benedict XVI*, Volumes IV/1 and 2, for the year 2008). Both grayish blue with rather small photos on the cover. One showed Pope Benedict kneeling, clothed entirely in white, at Ground Zero of the destroyed Twin Towers in Manhattan, New York, that iconic image of terror, which on September 11, 2001, opened a new and horrifying chapter of the apocalypse for mankind. And another showed him kneeling, in his red mozetta, in the grotto in Lourdes, where in 1858 [1844 (*sic*) = year of St. Bernadette's birth], over a wild rosebush growing from the crevice of a cliff, the Mother of God, wearing a white robe trimmed in blue with roses at her feet, had appeared eighteen times to the fourteen-year-old Bernadette Soubirous; during the third apparition on February 18, she had introduced herself with the words: "*Voulez-vous me faire la grâce de venir ici pendant quinze jours?*" ("Would you kindly do me the favor of coming here for fifteen days?")

On the books lay a sealed envelope with a short letter [in German] on heavy stationery that read as follows:

Dear Herr Badde,

Many thanks for your friendly letter on the Feast of Peter and Paul! I gladly send you, enclosed, the *Insegnamenti* from the year 2008, so that you can fill in the gap that was caused by your stroke. With cordial best wishes and my blessing on all your work and also for a well-deserved vacation,

Yours truly,
Benedict XVI

The signature, written with a thin, fine black pencil, was as clear and small as ever. It was even less of a scrawl than in recent years, and the old-fashioned abbreviation "PP." was missing. It was friendly, but not all that personal. The "Yours truly" was typed, not written by hand.

I looked at the books. Volume I (January to June 2008) has 1,279 pages, with a 164-page scholarly index. There were countless texts in all the languages of the world, including Polish, which Benedict XVI had learned at an advanced age out of respect for and as a sort of bow to his saintly predecessor. I looked for texts dated March 6, a Thursday on which I had had my stroke in the evening while shopping and suddenly could scarcely move my foot any more but only drag it along, as though my shoe were stuck on a gigantic piece of chewing gum that I had stepped on. That morning Benedict XVI had given a speech in Spanish to the bishops of Guatemala, who were visiting him in Rome, in which he shared their concern "about the increasing violence and heavy emigration" and "about the poverty that afflicts large segments of the population." This situation required the bishops to increase their efforts "to show to everyone the merciful Face of the Lord; in keeping with Her vocation, the

Church should be the image of that Face by serving and assisting the suffering and the weakest with generosity and dedication." He declared also to the Guatemalan bishops his solidarity in the "danger presented by the sects that are causing confusion," and he emphasized that their primary task is "the evangelization of cultures." Afterward he commended them "to Our Lady of the Rosary, the Patroness of Guatemala." Surely those shepherds flew back to their country strengthened afterward. Nevertheless, it was a papal routine by which they had been encouraged.

Volume II had 1,098 pages. Here the index began on page 953. I flipped back and forth: 1,279 plus 1,098 makes 2,377 pages as the output of a single year. *Insegnamenti* means approximately "lessons": 2,377 pages from a teacher who in that year, 2008, turned eighty-one, made me, as a former (but at that time much younger) teacher, feel dizzy. How did he manage it? His predecessor, John Paul II, had let the highly gifted Monsignor Sardi draft many of his many statements for him, and for this he was later rewarded with a cardinal's hat. Delegating his personal statements in this way was unthinkable in most cases for the nimble-minded, polyglot Pope from Germany. He could not help formulating by himself what he wanted and had to say, or at least rewriting and supplementing prepared texts. He was extremely reluctant to have someone else's words put into his mouth. His *insegnamenti* really should be his own *insegnamenti*. Not a word from his Jesus trilogy, which he was writing at the same time also, appeared in these two volumes. Naturally all this was not soon forgotten by many critics in the Roman Curia, as early as 2008, who thought that a Pope should govern and take care of all his many items of official business and no longer spend his hours at his desk on his work as a teacher. He himself, though, always recovered again and again in those hours at his desk from the stress of his difficult office.

And this letter was therefore — in July 2014 — his gentle answer to my request that he might "forward to me maybe three to five statements of any kind that you wrote that you consider especially important during that period of time." The fact that he sent me two fat volumes with a few friendly lines in response to my request for three statements was more eloquent than any other answer. *"Da schau her!"* [approximately: "Well, lookie here!"], he replied in the Bavarian dialect with this package. That was important for him in that year. Everything. It was as though he saw himself now — more than a year after his resignation — like a Doctor of the Church already: a *doctor ecclesiae*, like Saint Bonaventure (1212-1274) whom he revered so much, the *doctor seraphicus*, the "Seraphic Teacher" who as the seventh Minister General re-founded, as it were, the Franciscans of the truly chaotic early period thirty years after the death of Saint Francis, from whom we learned the following, for example: "On account of these three things God created the rational soul: that she might praise Him, that she might serve Him, that she might delight in Him and rest in Him; and this happens through love, for whoever abides in love, abides in God and God abides in him."

More than seven hundred years later, though, on April 18, 2008, the new "Doctor of the Church," Benedict, addressed not just the Catholic Church but the whole world, when in French and English he exhorted the members of the General Assembly of the United Nations in their glass palace on East River in New York City to understand that the acknowledgment of natural law is indispensable for the peaceful coexistence of "the family of nations." This highly complex, more than 3,000-word speech also reads in retrospect like a preliminary study for his later speech in the *Reichstag* in Berlin. But above all he revived here the "responsibility to protect," the ancient principle from international law, when he warned: "The founding of the United Nations, as we know, coincided with the profound upheavals that humanity experienced when reference to the meaning of transcendence and natural reason was abandoned, and in consequence, freedom and human dignity were grossly violated." It was a concept that eight years later was suddenly invoked again and again for preliminary solutions, so as to counter responsibly the terror regime of a caliphate in Syria and in Iraq. The founding of the United Nations Organization, which was accompanied by the "Universal Declaration of Human Rights," Benedict XVI declared on the East River, was:

> the outcome of a convergence of different religious and cultural traditions, all of them motivated by the common desire to place the human person at the heart of institutions, laws and the workings of society, and to consider the human person essential for the world of culture, religion and science. Human rights are increasingly being presented as the common language and the ethical substratum of international relations.... [These rights] are based on the natural law inscribed on human hearts and present in different cultures and civilizations. Removing human rights from this context would mean restricting their range and yielding to a relativistic conception, according to which the meaning and interpretation of rights could vary and their universality would be denied in the name of different cultural, political, social, and even religious outlooks. This great variety of viewpoints must not be allowed to obscure the fact that not only are rights universal, but so too is the human person, the subject of those rights.

For this speech about principles, the Pope from Bavaria quoted Augustine of Hippo from the fifth century as "one of the masters of our intellectual heritage," leading up to a prophetic plea for religious freedom as one of the new pillars of human rights:

> Human rights, of course, must include the right to religious freedom.... It should never be necessary to deny God in order to enjoy one's rights. The rights associated with religion are all the more in need of protection if they are considered to clash with a prevailing secular ideology or with majority religious positions of an exclusive nature.

He was tracing here the political reference points of his pontificate that he had outlined for the first time in his first New Year's address in 2005 to the diplomats accredited to the Vatican. He said goodbye to the representatives of the United Nations in the seven official languages of the U.N. and afterward hurried up the craggy backbone of Manhattan to the Park East Synagogue.

It was Friday, April 18, 2008. On that evening the Sabbath would begin, together with Passover, on which occasion he wanted to convey personally to the representatives of the largest Jewish congregation in the world, in New York, his greeting of peace and his best wishes for blessings. "Dear friends, Shalom! Blessed be the name of the Lord!" Exactly three years earlier he had been elected Pope. Now he presided that same evening also at an ecumenical meeting in Saint Joseph Church, and then celebrated Holy Mass on Saturday in Saint Patrick's Cathedral, met with a group of handicapped persons, and then with seminarians (with a speech in English and Spanish), before setting out early on Sunday, even before the big concluding Mass in Yankee Stadium, for a prayer at Ground Zero. The wind between

the skyscrapers billowed his cassock and those of his assistants
who held up for him here, on the edge of that abyss of horror,
an English prayer to read, which as always he recited without
pronouncing "th" correctly and here and there with the accent
on the wrong syllable, yet in a heartbreakingly soft and moving
tone of voice. Afterward he—being the smallest among all who
accompanied him—lit a candle and put it into a globe:

> O God of love, compassion, and healing, look on us,
> people of many different faiths and traditions, who
> gather today at this site, the scene of incredible violence
> and pain. We ask You in Your goodness to give eternal
> light and peace to all who died here—the heroic first-
> responders: our fire fighters, police officers, emergency
> service workers, and Port Authority personnel, along with
> all the innocent men and women who were victims of
> this tragedy simply because their work or service brought
> them here on September 11, 2001.
>
> We ask You, in Your compassion, to bring healing
> to those who, because of their presence here that day,
> suffer from injuries and illness. Heal, too, the pain of
> still-grieving families and all who lost loved ones in this
> tragedy. Give them strength to continue their lives with
> courage and hope. . . .
>
> God of peace, bring Your peace to our violent world:
> peace in the hearts of all men and women and peace
> among the nations of the earth. Turn to Your way of love
> those whose hearts and minds are consumed with hatred.
>
> God of understanding, overwhelmed by the magnitude
> of this tragedy, we seek Your light and guidance as we
> confront such terrible events. Grant that those whose

lives were spared may live so that the lives lost here may not have been lost in vain. Comfort and console us, strengthen us in hope, and give us the wisdom and courage to work tirelessly for a world where true peace and love reign among nations and in the hearts of all.

I watched the moving video on YouTube once again and continued to browse in the volumes. It was difficult to disengage myself from this chronicle of just one year and the wealth that it contains.

In 2008 Benedict XVI made three spectacular journeys to two different continents and within Europe. They were: this same trip to the United States and to the headquarters of the UN in New York (April 15-21), then a trip to far-off Sydney, Australia, for the World Youth Day (July 12-21), and finally a trip to France (September 12-15) on the occasion of the 150th anniversary of the appearances of the Mother of God in Lourdes. In addition there were forty-two General Audiences on Saint Peter's Square, in Paul VI Hall and in Castel Gandolfo in the presence of countless people. Bishops from all over the world came to visit him, more than twenty heads of state — all in all it was a superhuman schedule for an old man at an advanced age, and yet he tirelessly kept his appointments, and the records of them are compiled in the books that I am now holding. There were also four pastoral journeys within Italy: to Pompeii, to Cagliari on the island of Sardinia, to the southernmost tip of the peninsula to Santa Maria di Leuca and to Brindisi. Then up north to Savona and Genoa. As in Rome, not a day went by without meetings — which were always encounters also with the ever-new problems of the Catholic Church worldwide. It was too much.

And yet here too there were always hours in which all the ballast seemed suddenly to fall from him, for instance on Friday,

September 12, 2008, when he met in Paris at the Collège des Bernardins with representatives of the French cultural elite, among whom the Knight of the *"Légion d'honneur"* probably felt most at home outside of Bavaria. To no other language did his tongue ever adapt so well as to French. In that language he now gave a lecture about the birth of Europe "from the spirit of the search for God." It was a masterpiece from the workshop of the master thinker, in which he instructed secular Paris first about the fact that:

> amid the great cultural upheaval resulting from migrations of peoples and the emerging new political configurations, the monasteries were the places where the treasures of ancient culture survived, and where at the same time a new culture slowly took shape out of the old. But how did it happen? ... First and foremost, it must be frankly admitted straight away that it was not their intention to create a culture nor even to preserve a culture from the past. Their motivation was much more basic. Their goal was: *quaerere Deum* [to seek God]. Amid the confusion of the times, in which nothing seemed permanent, they wanted to do the essential — to make an effort to find what was perennially valid and lasting, life itself.

Therefore in monasticism, from the beginning, "the longing for God, the *désir de Dieu*, includes *amour des lettres*, love of the word [or literature], exploration of all its dimensions." Therefore "it was appropriate that the monastery should have a library, pointing out pathways to the word. It was also appropriate to have a school, in which these pathways could be opened up." And for prayer that issues from the word of God, speech is not enough: music is required." Christian worship, indeed, means accepting the invitation "an invitation to sing with the angels, [so as] to harmonize with the music of the noble spirits who were considered the originators of the harmony of the cosmos, the music of the spheres. . . . This intrinsic requirement of speaking with God and singing of Him with words He Himself has given, is what gave rise to the great tradition of Western music."

From here he made a transition to a short lesson about the character of the Bible, which, "considered from a purely histori-cal and literary perspective, is not simply a book, but a collection of literary texts which were redacted over the course of more than a thousand years, and in which the inner unity of the in-dividual books is not immediately apparent. On the contrary, there are visible tensions between them." Therefore:

> the New Testament generally designates the Bible not as "the Scripture" but as "the Scriptures," which, when taken together, are naturally then regarded as the one word of God to us. But the use of this plural makes it quite clear that the word of God only comes to us through the human word and through human words, that God only speaks to us through the humanity of human agents, through their words and their history.

Only in the dynamic unity of the whole are the many books therefore one single book, in which God's word and God's action is manifested in human history. "This tension between obligation and freedom, which extends far beyond the literary problem of scriptural exegesis," was decisive for the thought and the work of monasticism also and made a profound mark on Western culture.

However, a second component was added, which really made monasticism an essential supporting pillar of European history. For "in the Greek world, manual labour was considered something for slaves." There, the wise man, the truly free man was devoted solely to intellectual things. He left manual work, as something base, to men who are not capable of this higher life in the world of the mind. "The Jewish tradition was quite different: all the great rabbis practised at the same time some form of handcraft.... Monasticism took up this tradition." This was the origin of the extraordinary Benedictine motto, "*Ora et labora.*" ("Pray and work.") Besides prayer, work—and in particular manual work—belonged and belongs in every case to Christian monasticism from the beginning as a constituent element.

> The Graeco-Roman world did not have a creator God; according to its vision, the highest divinity could not, as it were, dirty his hands in the business of creating matter.... The Christian God is different: He, the one, real and only God, is also the Creator. God is working.... Thus human work was now seen as a special form of human resemblance to God, as a way in which man can and may share in God's activity as Creator of the world. Monasticism involves not only a culture of the word, but also a culture of work, without which the emergence of Europe, its ethos and its influence on the world would be unthinkable.

For like Paul and the first Christians, the monks were imbued with the conviction that "the God in whom they believed was the God of all people, the one, true God, who had revealed Himself in the history of Israel and ultimately in His Son, thereby supplying the answer which was of concern to everyone and for which all people, in their innermost hearts, are waiting." And "that at the beginning of all things, there must be not irrationality, but creative Reason—not blind chance, but freedom."

Although all human beings somehow know this, as Paul wrote in his Letter to the Romans, this knowledge remains unreal:

> [A] God who is merely imagined and invented is not God at all. If He does not reveal Himself, we cannot gain access to Him. The novelty of Christian proclamation is that it can now say to all peoples: He has revealed Himself. He personally.... The novelty of Christian proclamation does not consist in a thought, but in a deed: God has revealed Himself.... Creation (*factum*) is rational.

With the following words he concluded the speech, and it met with overwhelming applause: "What gave Europe's culture its foundation—the search for God and the readiness to listen to Him—remains today the basis of any genuine culture. To seek God and let ourselves be found by Him is no less necessary today than in past times. *Merci*."

This then was the sort of thing in the *Insegnamenti* that the retired Benedict XVI sent to me six years after the fact—in the year 2014. Throughout his life you could tell that he had a great fascination with monasticism. That was why after his election to the papacy he did not call himself John Paul III but Benedict XVI, taking the name of the patriarch of Western monasticism. That was also why finally—as his strength abandoned him—he would retire on February 28, 2013, into a monk-like existence. But he had not reached that point yet in 2008, when only one day later he gave what was perhaps the most moving speech of the whole year. It was not a lecture but rather a story, not recounted in the presence of the intelligentsia of France, but told to poor and sick pilgrims, over a sea of candles, at the foot of the Pyrenees during the torchlight procession of the sick and the abandoned in Lourdes. Because these words were so lyrical, it is fitting to reprint them in these notes, in slightly abridged form.

"One hundred and fifty years ago, on 11 February 1858," he began cautiously in a slightly raspy voice,

in this place known as the Grotto of Massabielle, away from the town, a simple young girl from Lourdes, Bernadette Soubirous, saw a light, and in this light she saw a young lady who was "beautiful, more beautiful than any other." This woman addressed her with kindness and gentleness, with respect and trust: "She said *vous* to me [*i.e.* used the polite form of address in French]," Bernadette recounted, "Would you do me the kindness of coming here for a fortnight?" the Lady asked her. "She was looking at me as one person who speaks to another." It was in this conversation, in this dialogue marked by such delicacy, that the Lady instructed her to deliver certain very simple messages on prayer, penance and conversion. It is hardly surprising that Mary should be beautiful, given that—during the apparition of 25 March 1858—she reveals her name in this way: "I am the Immaculate Conception." ...

The Most Holy Virgin Mary ... wears on her head a crown of twelve stars which represent the twelve tribes of Israel, the entire people of God, the whole communion of saints, while at her feet is the moon, image of death and mortality. Mary left death behind her; she is entirely re-clothed with life, the life of her Son, the risen Christ.... Countless people have borne witness to this: when they encountered Bernadette's radiant face, it left a deep impression on their hearts and minds. Whether it was during the apparitions themselves or while she was recounting them, her face was simply shining. Bernadette from that time on had the light of Massabielle dwelling within her. The daily life of the Soubirous family was nevertheless a tale of deprivation and sadness, sickness and incomprehension, rejection and poverty. Even if there was no lack of love and warmth in family relationships, life at the *cachot* [a former dungeon] was hard. Nevertheless, the shadows of the earth did not prevent the light of heaven from shining. "The light shines in the darkness ..." (John 1:5).

Lourdes is one of the places chosen by God for His beauty to be reflected with particular brightness, hence the importance here of the symbol of light. From the fourth apparition onwards, on arriving at the grotto, Bernadette would light a votive candle each morning and hold it in her left hand for as long as the Virgin was visible to her. Soon, people would give Bernadette a candle to plant in the ground inside the grotto. Very soon, too, people would place their own candles in this place of light and peace. The Mother of God herself let it be known that she liked the touching homage of these thousands of torches, which since that time have continued to shine upon the rock of the apparition and give her glory. From that day, before the grotto, night and day, summer and winter, a burning bush shines out, aflame with the prayers of pilgrims and the sick, who bring their concerns and their needs, but above all their faith and their hope.

By coming here to Lourdes on pilgrimage, we wish to enter, following in Bernadette's footsteps, into this extraordinary closeness between heaven and earth, which never fails and never ceases to grow. In the course of the apparitions, it is notable that Bernadette prays the rosary under the gaze of Mary, who always joined in and prayed along when Bernadette recited the formula: "Glory be to the Father and to the Son and to the Holy Spirit, as it was in the beginning, is now and ever shall be, world without end. Amen." This is the so-called doxology, as theologians call this prayer, that the young Mother of God always prayed together with little Bernadette. This fact confirms the profoundly theocentric character of the prayer of the rosary. When we pray it, Mary offers us her heart and her gaze in order to contemplate the life of her Son, Jesus Christ....

The torchlight procession expresses the mystery of prayer in a form that our eyes of flesh can grasp: in the communion of the Church, which unites the elect in heaven with pilgrims on earth, the light of dialogue between man and his Lord blazes forth and a luminous path opens up in human history, even in its darkest moments. This procession is a time of great ecclesial joy, but also a time of seriousness: the intentions we bring emphasize our profound communion with all those who suffer.... How can our life not be transformed by this? Why should our whole life and being not become places of hospitality for our neighbours? Lourdes is a place of light because it is a place of communion, hope and conversion.... We need light, and at the same time are called to be light....

The apparitions were bathed in light and God chose to ignite in Bernadette's gaze a flame which converted countless hearts.... To live Christian love, means at the same time to introduce God's light into the world and to point out its true source....

In this shrine at Lourdes, to which the Christians of the whole world have turned their gaze since the Virgin Mary caused hope and love to shine here by giving pride of place to the sick, the poor and the little ones, we are invited to discover the simplicity of our vocation: *Il suffit d'aimer* [It is enough to love].

Night had fallen. Around the Pope a sea of lights glowed. The next day, on Sunday, September 14, 2008, he would give here in Lourdes five more major, fundamental homilies and speeches to believing and unbelieving, secular France—and to the sick and the suffering. In the *Insegnamenti* they take up thirty-seven pages in all (pages 301-338). Afterward he flew on Monday back to Rome, where on Wednesday in his General Audience in Paul VI Hall he reflected once again on the spiritual proceeds of his journey. Four years later, though, when he looked for a suitable date for the spectacular announcement of his resignation, he did not choose for it the memorial of Augustine or Bonaventure, the Doctors of the Church whom he revered so much, but rather February 11, the Catholic "memorial of Our Lady of Lourdes." In the year 1858 the "Lady" first appeared to little Bernadette on the bank of the Gave River and the girl only looked. The day of her death was April 16, 1879. Exactly forty-eight years later Joseph Ratzinger was born in Marktl am Inn.

Brouhaha about the Society of Saint Pius X, and Pilgrim in the Holy Land — 2009

Steep cliffs to climb—Rome, January 18, 2009
The Sistine Chapel is a chamber of transformation. It is the room of the Last Judgment, in which Joseph Ratzinger disappeared in April 2005, only to emerge as the new Pope, Benedict XVI, in the Sala Regia of the Vatican. On Saturday evening, however, Benedict XVI had turned back again for an hour or so in that fateful chamber. There, suddenly he became Joseph again, Georg's younger brother, who had just turned eighty-five. In his honor, the *Domspatzen* from the cathedral in Regensburg performed Mozart's C-minor Mass in the Sistine Chapel, an incredibly beautiful fragment that the cathedral *Kapellmeister* Georg Ratzinger, though a passionate fan of Mozart, had never attempted during his time (1964-1995) as director of this oldest boys' choir in the world, out of sheer reverence.

In the evening of his life, now, the most splendid music and the most exquisite painting united for him in the Sistine Chapel, that unique instrument of world culture. The dark-sounding

Mass was a sort of key signature for their career as priests, the younger brother explained after the performance in a rare moment of public familiarity. These difficult tones with their gloomy dissonances had been "woven into" their life: the two brothers had heard this Mass setting for the first time in 1941 and had discovered its liberating beauty in that apocalyptic time. Now, in new days of "unprecedented violence," the Mozart fan on the papal throne was suddenly transformed again and spoke freely — in an artistic language that once was a distinctive trait of Joseph Ratzinger, which nevertheless he is almost always prevented from using in any public place, where unfortunately he can hardly ever speak without a prepared text.

"Our parents had just lost everything when you were born, dear Georg," he said. Then he reminded his brother of the "steep cliffs and dark passages" of the journey on which the two of them were traveling toward the "wedding feast of the Bride," where one day they might "enter into the heavenly concert" (after "a few more good years," he prayed, for his brother too).

An echo of this heavenly concert, nevertheless, had already been heard by all the guests, when Simona Šaturowá's voice again and again carried the "*et incarnatus est*" aloft to Michelangelo's Christ on the front wall, more perfectly than a violin could ever have done. The proclamation of the Incarnation of God is the most tender part of the Christian Creed. Here the fragment of Mozart's Mass mysteriously breaks off. Did he realize that he was incapable of continuing to compose this praise of God at such a high level? No one knows.

In the Sistine Chapel, though, it was as if all the guests were invited also to the transformation of a piece of music into a sung proof of the existence of God. All the laws of evolution cannot explain this marvelous work by Mozart; more plausibly, it can be understood only through a childlike faith in a Creator God.

Bishop run amok — Rome, January 25, 2009

Anti-Semitism is not only reprehensible but also socially suicidal, if it is advertised publicly. Denying the Holocaust is a punishable offense in Germany, plain and simple. Bishop Richard Williamson from England therefore knew exactly what he was doing when, with almost diabolical genius and flair, he traveled to the Diocese of Regensburg, the former home of Joseph Ratzinger, to give an interview in which he denied the Holocaust. For last week Cardinal Re signed also in Rome a document in which Benedict XVI ordered the lifting of the excommunication of four bishops whom Archbishop Lefebvre had illegally consecrated in 1988. Richard Williamson is one of them.

The Pope's dramatic step toward reconciliation is nevertheless extremely odious to him. So he responded to it with this interview, which cannot be understood in any other way but as the attempted suicide of an obdurate old man, so as to torpedo the reconciliation once again at the last moment. He thereby insulted the Pope, his three brother bishops, many believers, and Jewish communities throughout the world. Nevertheless, by doing so he could not prevent the lifting of the excommunication. It remains a purely canonical procedure, by which the Pope intends to dry up also the sectarian climate in which such pathologies thrive. The matter has nothing to do with the madness of the bishop run amok. Anyone who now becomes indignant with Benedict XVI would therefore be well advised to take another look at the confederate by whom he is letting himself be exploited in this matter.

Benedict Up Close

The Pope, the pallium, and the
Good Shepherd—Rome, February 1, 2009

Benedict XVI is "beside himself" [*entrückt*], readers of *Der Spiegel* know as of today. The man is actually blaming the Catholic Church. Yet hasn't the Pope gone completely out of his mind [*verrückt*] — not: *entrückt!* — leaving his large flock alone for the sake of a splinter group on the far-right fringe of the Church, and thus thoughtlessly putting at risk the long path of reconciliation with the Jews? That, essentially, is the critique of commentators ranging from Rabbi Homolka to Heiner Geissler, the former maverick of the CDU [Christian Democratic Union, a German political party], as they confided it to *Der Spiegel*. So for a moment now we should not talk about all the disasters that accompanied the lifting of the excommunication of the four bishops of the Society of Saint Pius X (which of course puts all political correctness to scorn), and instead take a look at the Pope's pallium. [*sic.* An intentionally funny line in German, twitting the *ad hominem*'s leveled at the Holy Father.] Besides his shepherd's staff and fisherman's ring, the pallium is one of the insignia of his office, which year after year is conferred on archbishops throughout the world. It is the woolen stole over his shoulders, for which he blesses young lambs every January 21 in the Roman Basilica of Saint Agnes, whose wool is shorn afterward in the Basilica of Saint Cecilia and woven into palliums, which are meant to remind him and all bishops of the words of Jesus that Luke quotes as follows: "What man of you, having a hundred sheep, if he has lost one of them, does not leave the ninety-nine in the wilderness, and go after the one which is lost, until he finds it?" The pallium symbolizes nothing other than the lost lamb, which the "good shepherd" carries back on his shoulders. And Benedict XVI has now done just that. He imitated the Good Shepherd when he briefly left his flock standing in the mountains in order to res-cue a single stray lamb that had remained caught somewhere in the thorn bushes and was in danger of being lost. That may be scarcely comprehensible nowadays. Certainly the step was not at all media-savvy. Nevertheless, it is genuinely Christian and probably shows the original, genuine face of the Church better and more attractively than many more agreeable steps. Benedict XVI did what he had to do — and that is a good thing.

Worst-case scenario in the "Sacri Palazzi" — Rome, February 4, 2009

Just when Benedict XVI needed his private secretary the most, Georg Gänswein was lying in bed with a fever. A flu had prostrated Don Giorgio. Gänswein is not a Curial Cardinal or a chief advi-sor to the Pope, yet the prelate is something like the Pope's right hand and his ultimate bodyguard. He must protect the Pontiff from being smothered with petitions and filter out the important messages from the unimportant ones. For three days in January he could not perform this duty. Was it a higher power? Probably. In any event it was the worst-case scenario, a perfect storm that had been brewing in recent days over the pontificate of Benedict XVI on the papal throne. Enough material for a new *Chronicle of a Death Foretold*. But so far no one has died in this disaster. The Pope neither declared a war nor started one. The mainstream media offer minute-by-minute updates, but the most fantastic theories circulate worldwide about what the affair actually was and is.

As the week began, there was talk in the newspaper *Il Gior-nale* about a mysterious "dossier" that was causing unrest behind the walls of the "Sacred Palaces." Many in the Vatican have heard about it. No one claims to have read it. The gist of the paper in front of us is the assertion that the Pope had been led by a minutely detailed timetable into a trap that had been set for him, into which he finally stumbled unawares. The paper ends of course with questions, not with answers. It does not say who was responsible for the coincidence between the lifting of the excommunication of four illicit bishops and the publication of the reckless statements of "Bishop" Williamson.

"Ignorant sloppiness and a lack of communication in the Curia" led to this catastrophe, many Vatican watchers maintain. The Pope "fell into the rapids while building a bridge." Slipshod work had been done, especially in the Pontifical Commission *Ecclesia Dei*. "No," retorts Msgr. Camille Perl, the Vice President of this Pontifical Commission headed by the Columbian Cardinal Hoyos. "The four bishops of the Society of Saint Pius X had repeatedly asked the Pope to lift the excommunication against them. They understood this to be the second '*préalable*,' as they said, a sort of prerequisite, so as to begin then joint discussions about overcoming the schism that had unfortunately occurred." For Benedict XVI had already granted an initial demand that the Pope should again allow Mass to be celebrated in the rite that was in force in the Latin Church until 1970, since this too was according to his wishes.

> For the sake of unity he therefore decided to "pardon" these four bishops too, in response to the petition that they had repeatedly submitted. This act pertained only to the lifting of the excommunication. Therefore there was no special investigation into their private lives or political views. After all, this was not the appointment of a new bishop, but the readmission of bishops who were

already consecrated. The fact that a British eccentric was among them — or what he thought — simply had not occurred to anyone. We do not work here in the way that French conspiracy theorists imagine. Anyone who thinks so vastly overestimates Rome.

Besides, a long process had preceded the decision to pardon. The overwhelming majority of the cardinals had already agreed to the step in late 2007. "It was always clear that another process of dialogue was to follow it, in which there will be discussion of the difficulties that until now have kept these bishops away from full communion with the Catholic Church."

Consequently, the Pope could not have dreamed who was among these bishops until he woke up to a nightmare. For in a way the bishops had even been "downgraded" by his act to a status in which they initially no longer had any episcopal ministry but were to be regarded as simple Christians, to whom, among other things, the Sacrament of Penance should no longer be refused. "Yes, we spoke above all with Bishop Fellay," Cardinal Hoyos told *Il Corriere della Sera* last week, "the General Superior of the Society, and until the last moment of this dialogue we knew absolutely nothing about this Williamson. When I handed the signed Decree to *Monseigneur* Fellay, we knew nothing about this [videotaped] interview." No one in the Vatican had googled the bishops.

Meanwhile, outside the Vatican walls, that explanation is considered "ivory tower," for instance by the Jesuit Klaus Mertes from Berlin, who with that expression means the labyrinth of "bureaucratic offices" that even Alfred Delp had warned about, before the Nazis executed him. But that was not all. "One problem was that they had spoken almost exclusively with Bishop Fellay," says one high-ranking prelate in the Secretariat of State.

There was wrangling over competencies. We had information available about Bishop Williamson as of January 22. We did all we could to prevent the document from being made public on the 24th. Granted, on January 21 the signature was already on the document; nevertheless a postponement would have been possible. There had already been postponements in the past. For the document was not well thought-out either; it left the canonical position unclear.

Besides Hoyos, the one responsible, who was in a hurry, the Cardinal Secretary of State Bertone was reportedly "relatively guarded" in the matter. Cardinal Levada, however, the head of the Congregation for the Doctrine of the Faith, had just returned to his desk again weakened after suffering a slipped disc. So the many petitions were of no use. On January 24, early in the morning, an e-mail from England arrived at the Vatican, which read: "If the Pope wants to lift the excommunication, after Williamson denied the Holocaust, the Pope's enemies will try to destroy him. We are on the verge of a catastrophe. Doesn't Msgr. Gänswein know it?"

The Pope knew nothing about it. Monsignor Gänswein probably knew it. But he was sick in bed. It was midday on that rainy Saturday in Rome, when at around 12:00 a dry communiqué that announced the lifting of the excommunication was distributed in the press room of the "Holy See." Not many journalists scrambled after it. In the winter days that followed, the news was like a little snowball that only a week later had swelled into an avalanche barreling down on Saint Peter's.

Was complete miscalculation behind it? Certainly. Yet there is no need for a conspiracy theory to recognize here also a concatenation of the most unfortunate circumstances that caused the Pope to stumble into this doomsday scenario. In his General Audience on Wednesday he no longer mentioned the case at all, but rather explained the conclusion of the Second Letter to Timothy by the Apostle Paul: "I have fought the good fight, I have finished the race, I have kept the faith." Did he perhaps consider the case already closed, as Cardinal Secretary of State Bertone did? Minutes later a clarification was issued by the Secretariat of State which said: "In order to be admitted to function as a Bishop within the Church, Bishop Williamson must also distance himself in an absolutely unequivocal and public way from his positions regarding the *Shoah,* which were unknown to the Holy Father at the time of the remission of the excommunication."

Identity and continuity — Rome, February 11, 2009

The obelisk on Saint Peter's Square weighs about 3,000 metric tons and is 4,000 years old. Caligula had it brought from Egypt to Rome around the year A.D. 40 and set it up beside the Vatican Hill, on the Circus of Gaius. It stood there for more than one and a half millennia. Only its surroundings changed from one era to the next. For a long time a bronze ball decorated the top — it was said to contain Caesar's ashes — and when it was opened in 1586 they found a bit of dust and earth in it. That was the same year in which the obelisk, in a feat of engineering, was brought from its former location beside the basilica on the left to its present site. Bernini's Saint Peter's Square did not yet exist, not even the present-day façade of Saint Peter's. Since then the gigantic stone has been adorned with a cross, which preserves fragments of the "true Cross" that Helena, the mother of Emperor Constantine, discovered in Jerusalem in 325 A.D.

In its new location, the obelisk is now a calendar stone, which always casts the longest shadow of the year exactly on the winter solstice on the degree of latitude that runs over the Square toward the Apostolic Palace, in which the popes resided in recent centuries. But when Benedict XVI steps to his window Sunday after Sunday to pray the Angelus, he must always see in the obelisk also a sort of celestial sundial. For the mysterious stone with no inscription on which his glance falls again and again is like a mirror that received the last glance of the Apostle Peter 2,000 years ago. When Peter, the predecessor of all popes, was crucified head-down during the reign of Nero two hundred meters further on at the edge of the Circus, he looked at this obelisk. The Vatican Hill at that time had become Golgotha for Peter. This view from above therefore allows—even despite all criticism from below—an excellent view of a mirror of the Petrine office and two central concepts of the Church of Rome. They are *identity* and *continuity*.

For the Pope, the Church is not just an identical unity in the local and historical sense; he is also the primary guarantor of that unity for Her. The Universal Church is not only anchored in the center of societies, but is also rooted in the depths of history. This is why in a risky venture he tried to win back the most recent schismatics in history out of that brooding sectarian climate for the Church Universal, from which they had strayed since they split off around thirty years ago. For even talk about a "pre-conciliar" and a "post-conciliar" Church was intolerable to Joseph Ratzinger. Finally, for Benedict XVI, this sort of talk deep down is no less heretical than the grumblings [*das Giften*] of the schismatics. No Council in history was ever preceded by talk about "pre-conciliar" and "post-conciliar," a pair of terms with unmistakably ideological overtones—whereby "post-conciliar" suddenly stood for everything imaginable that was progressive and good, and "pre-conciliar" stood for what was backward, stupid and simply bad. We cannot forbid the Pope, as the *Pontifex Maximus*, to consider the rift made by such an artificial division as problematic. For also connoted by these categories is a departure from the unity of identity and continuity, and likewise a departure from the awareness that the Church has to defend an ever-endangered unity not only today (in a social sense) but also Her unity through the ages, in a historical as well as an eternal sense—since a large part of the Church has long since dwelled no longer on earth but in the next world. This is the only reason why relics are embedded in every altar.

After all, not only is the foundation of the Church by Christ "pre-conciliar," but so are all the Apostles and almost all Saints—from Saint Cecilia down to Edith Stein, "the outstanding daughter of Israel and true daughter of the Church," as John Paul II called her. Therefore the Pope from the land of the Reformation, of all people, had to try urgently, as "Supreme Bridge-builder," to bridge this rift in our awareness and our talk between the "pre-conciliar" and the "post-conciliar" period. He did nothing else in his attempt to start over again carefully with the Society of Saint Pius X. He is quite familiar with their militant rejection of many aspects of the Council, since he himself, like hardly any other living bishop, was a key figure in the Council. But therefore he is also especially conscious of the fact that the Church was by no means newly invented in the last Council. She does not have to arrive laboriously in the present. She has always been there already. Or does somebody seriously want to exclude the Church from the brave new world of modernity? She does not have to worry at all therefore about Her timeliness. It is more difficult to guarantee that the connection to the beginning does not tear, to the Cenacle in Jerusalem. Therefore was it not consistent that Benedict XVI—after extending his hand shortly after his election to Hans Küng and inviting the agnostic Jewish author Oriana Fallaci to Castel Gandolfo—sought ecumenical dialogue with the schismatic Society of Saint Pius X also? Wasn't he allowed to and supposed to do that? Should he no longer pursue ecumenism with the Protestants just because Dr. Martin Luther also said unspeakable things about the Jews? Did Benedict XVI perhaps forget even one word of all that he has said about Christianity being radically rooted in Judaism? To ask these questions is to answer them. The continuity of the Church out of Judaism looms for Benedict XVI in the history of Europe like the obelisk on Saint Peter's Square towers to the sky. Therefore "the Roman Church has always protected the Jews too," wrote Valeriu Marcu in 1934 while fleeing from the Nazis, "so that people might keep a sacred thread of memory in times of ever-recurring barbarism that announce that history begins with them." This statement could have come from Joseph Ratzinger too. He will never go back to before the Council—yet he wants to and also will keep trying persistently to put together again what belongs together.

New Letter to the Galatians—Rome, March 11, 2009

The Pope heard nothing on January 24 when a bomb went off under his window, nor did he dream that the worst weeks of his pontificate might begin that very day, four days after he had extended his hand to validly but illicitly consecrated bishops in a "discreet gesture of mercy." Benedict XVI must have been shocked in the following days to see how an "avalanche of protests was unleashed, whose bitterness laid bare wounds deeper than those of the present moment." Was he paralyzed? He was probably saddened most of all, "that even Catholics who, after all, might have had a better knowledge of the situation, thought they had to attack me with open hostility." But he did not say that until fifty days later, in a moving letter to all the bishops of the Catholic Church, in which he now, after a long silence, explains the events of recent weeks from his perspective, so as "to contribute to peace in the Church." For of course there could be no more talk of that in recent days.

The idea for the letter occurred to the Pope on February 20, after he had explained in the Major Seminary of the Diocese of Rome a passage from the Apostle Paul's Letter to the Galatians, which also talked about an extremely vehement dispute even in the earliest days of the Church (which even prompted Paul to remark that all those who were causing unrest in the community, with the claim that Paul continued to demand Jewish circumcision of the newly baptized, should go ahead and "mutilate themselves"). "For you were called to freedom," Paul exclaimed to the Galatians back then, and now the Pope added:

> Since the beginning and throughout all time but especially in the modern age freedom has been the great dream of humanity. We know that Luther was inspired by this passage from the Letter to the Galatians and that he concluded that the monastic Rule, the hierarchy, the Magisterium seemed to him as a yoke of slavery from which it was necessary to liberate oneself. Subsequently, the Age of Enlightenment was totally guided, penetrated, by this desire for freedom, which was considered to have finally been reached. But Marxism too presented itself as a road towards freedom.

From the beginning in Christianity there have been very vehement debates and misunderstandings about the correct concept and use of freedom, which is why Paul warned the Galatians as early as the first century: "If you bite and devour one another take heed that you are not consumed by one another." Even Paul therefore alluded back then to polemics "that are born where faith degenerates into intellectualism and humility is replaced with the arrogance of being better than the other." Everyone could see very well that something similar is happening today, Benedict XVI said now. "Is it surprising that we too are no better than the Galatians?" he then asked. "That at least we are beset by the same temptations? That we must learn again and again how to use freedom correctly?"

Therefore it was not the critique of the German Federal Chancellor, not the protest of German theologians, nor even the statement by the Shepherds (who in recent days often went after each other more with their crooks than after the wolves lurking around their flocks), but rather this document from the earliest period of the Church that gave the Pope the idea in February to compose a "Letter to the Galatians" too, in which he would comprehensively tell all the bishops his views about the troubles of recent weeks, with all the mistakes that were made, which he frankly admits—and to explain in its entirety the complicated procedure of lifting the excommunication of the four illicitly consecrated bishops. With a similar letter two years ago he had already accompanied the reinstatement of the old Tridentine Rite. To say that the new letter comes fifty days too late therefore misses the mark somewhat. For no one could possibly have anticipated the conflict which, through the controversy over the Society of Saint Pius X, has meanwhile, like barium meal, exposed many fault lines within the Church. The fact that others made the mistakes for which he takes responsibility, and yet he does not want their heads to roll, gives us a glimpse into the artisanal production of such a letter by Benedict XVI. Indeed, to this day the eighty-one-year-old has no political correctness. Even as a professor he did not write on a typewriter. Rather, now as always, he takes a sharpened pencil and a white sheet of paper, and always writes — as with his books — "as regularly and with the same concentration as a woman who takes up her knitting again," and dictates [*sic*]: "Dear Brothers in the Episcopal Ministry — Exclamation point — The remission of the excommunication of the four Bishops consecrated in 1988 by Archbishop Lefebvre without a mandate of the Holy See has for many reasons caused — comma — both within and beyond the Catholic Church — comma — a discussion more heated than any we have seen for a long time — period — Many Bishops felt perplexed by an event which came about unexpectedly and was difficult to view positively in the light of the issues and tasks facing the Church today." A little further on he continues self-critically: "I have been told that consulting the information available on the internet would have made it possible to perceive the problem early on. I have learned the lesson that in the future in the Holy See we will have to pay greater attention to that source of news."

No one can expect that now Benedict XVI himself will soon be surfing on the Internet. He will keep writing with a pencil, as he did this time, when he said to the bishops, among other things, the following:

> An unforeseen mishap for me was the fact that the Williamson case came on top of the remission of the excommunication. The discreet gesture of mercy towards four Bishops ordained validly but not legitimately suddenly appeared as something completely different: as the

repudiation of reconciliation between Christians and Jews, and thus as the reversal of what the Council had laid down in this regard to guide the Church's path. A gesture of reconciliation with an ecclesial group engaged in a process of separation thus turned into its very antithesis: an apparent step backwards with regard to all the steps of reconciliation between Christians and Jews taken since the Council—steps which my own work as a theologian had sought from the beginning to take part in and support. That this overlapping of two opposed processes took place and momentarily upset peace between Christians and Jews, as well as peace within the Church, is something which I can only deeply deplore.

The Pope—in agreement with many rabbis—now characterizes this artificially concocted crisis in the Jewish-Christian dialogue as only "momentary"; many perhaps will hold this too against him even after this letter.

He then says: "Another mistake, which I deeply regret, is the fact that the extent and limits of the provision of 21 January 2009 were not clearly and adequately explained at the moment of its publication." He goes on to describe the complex procedure of an excommunication and its possible remission, which he, as a sort of chess move, undertook in order to force the increasingly schismatic Society of Saint Pius X finally to engage in an absolutely necessary debate about the doctrine of the Church and of all Her Councils. As a concrete step therefore he intends to place the exchange with the Society under the competence of the Congregation for the Doctrine of the Faith, that is, the Magisterial office of the Universal Church. Cardinal Hoyos, who until now was responsible for the negotiations, is consequently out of the picture. He unmistakably accuses the Society of Saint Pius X of "arrogance and presumptuousness, an obsession with one-sided positions." Nevertheless, he is unwilling casually to let their priestly fraternity (with its "491 priests, 215 seminarians, 6 seminaries, 88 schools, 2 university-level institutes, 117 religious brothers, 164 religious sisters") "drift farther from the Church." For even their bitter opponents within the Church, "who put themselves forward as great defenders of the Council also need to be reminded that Vatican II embraces the entire doctrinal history of the Church. Anyone who wishes to be obedient to the Council has to accept the faith professed over the centuries, and cannot sever the roots from which the tree draws its life."

He had already pointedly remarked to the Roman seminarians on February 20 that "in the discontinuity of the exterior events" in the Church there is still also "the great continuity of Her unity in every age." More moving than such reflections, however, are the passages in which the leader of Catholics exclaims almost imploringly:

> Was it, and is it, truly wrong in this case to meet half-way the brother who "has something against you" (cf. Matt. 5:23ff) and to seek reconciliation? Should not civil society also try to forestall forms of extremism and to incorporate their eventual adherents—to the extent possible—in the great currents shaping social life, and thus avoid their being segregated, with all its consequences?

He also becomes unsettling when he speaks about the impression:

> that our society needs to have at least one group to which no tolerance may be shown; which one can easily

attack and hate. And should someone dare to approach them — in this case the Pope — he too loses any right to tolerance; he too can be treated hatefully, without misgiving or restraint.

Hatred for the Pope? In recent days no one has spoken openly about that, although it was palpable everywhere. This is nevertheless not a plaintive letter of an old man, just because he frankly admits here how much he was affected by the campaign that was unleashed against him after the Williamson affair. The letter is described as "humble, surprising and strong" by an anonymous author in Rome in the Wednesday issue of *Il Foglio*, which first published in advance parts of it that had been leaked. Never has anyone read a letter like this from this Pope. In it he opens his heart. He emerges from his office as an individual, fragile person and shows that he does very much feel the blows and calumnies that are raining down on him. He does not want to speak about a martyrdom. More than a letter about hatred and love, however, this document is an apocalyptic and prophetic letter: it could be breathtaking for both his critics and his supporters to hear the old Pope speak here about "this moment of our history" in which "God is disappearing from the human horizon, and, with the dimming of the light which comes from God, humanity is losing its bearings, with increasingly evident destructive effects."

What is central to the letter, therefore, is not the reacquisition of the sacred, not the preservation of tradition, not the bridging of that fatal rift between a so-called pre-conciliar and a post-conciliar Church, but rather the faith itself, which he tries once more with this letter to explain anew to the bishops worldwide, "in our days, when in vast areas of the world the faith is in danger of dying out like a flame which no longer has fuel." In this hour, "the overriding priority is to make God present in this world and to show men and women the way to God. Not just any god, but the God who spoke on Sinai; to that God whose Face we recognize in a love which presses 'to the end' (cf. John 13:1) — in Jesus Christ, crucified and risen."

Westerners in the Levant — Amman, May 10, 2009

Jordan lies between Israel and Iraq. As early as the first century the land offered very young Christianity an initial refuge against the persecutions of the Romans. The Christians were here six hundred years before the Muslims, Prince Ghazi bin Muhammad bin Talal had impressed upon the Pope yesterday when the little successor of Peter visited the tall royal descendant of the Prophet in the big new mosque. This was the Pope's first and second day on his pilgrimage to the Levant, "which witnessed the preaching and the miracles of the Messiah, his death and his resurrection, and the outpouring of the Holy Spirit on the Church, so that it might become a sacrament of a reconciled, renewed humanity."

The Pope and his Muslim counterpart did not exchange any-thing — at least none of their dogmas and convictions, which are so close and at the same time extremely different. The respectful encounters of the Pope with the royal family and especially the meeting with Prince Ghazi nevertheless were reminiscent also of medieval — and altogether peaceful — miniatures in which a thoughtful priest listens to the victorious Saladin, the "noble knight" of the Muslims, who dealt the Crusaders from the West a devastating blow, but also taught them the art of playing chess, before sending them back home. For this reason, too, the Pope began his trip in Jordan. There are few places of the Islamic world where he could encounter a more open and enlightened side of Islam than in Jordan. We are here on the East Bank of the Jordan, in a mountain chain full of the peaks typical of this region of the world, which from dim, prehistoric times has formed a unit where things that belong together constantly crowd together. The Pope has not been able to hold off from this, his most dramatic pilgrimage to date, the fact that this unity is terribly torn. Pale desert light welcomed him in Amman. The day before an icy wind had blown over Jordan's capital, which is built of the same stone as Jerusalem on the other side of the Jordan Valley, only 4,000 years younger. His first steps still seemed hesitant. But then the Pope gathered speed with his crowded schedule for the country that derives its name from the water in which Jesus of Nazareth was baptized.

Fouad Twal, the new Latin Patriarch of the Church in the Holy Land, who is accompanying the Pope, is originally from Madaba, east of the Jordan Valley, where now, "confident in the gift of freedom," a laboratory for "mature faith" is to be set up in a new Christian university. In this region of the world "mature faith" is probably most urgently needed. For Jordan's King Abdullah II is — right in the middle of neighboring Israel! — still the protector of the Temple Mount in Jerusalem, which for 1,400 years has accommodated the third-holiest shrine of Islam, on exactly the same ground on which King Solomon 3,000 years ago had the first Temple of the Jews constructed. These are only a few of the tensions in that region, which the Pope intends in the next days to travel through as fearlessly as Peter (after Christ's resurrection!).

The thing about these first days that may perhaps linger in memory more than his speeches, though, is the picture that the stressed old Pope presents to Prince Ghazi as an auditor and a listener, when he greeted him in the big new mosque in Arabic and Latin: "*Salam aleikum! Pax vobis!*" The stronghold of faith quotes in several of its architectural details the famous Mezquita de Córdoba, which the Spaniards, over the course of the Christian re-conquest of the Iberian Peninsula almost a thousand years ago, transformed from a mosque into a cathedral. Now the mosque itself became the house in which the third visit of a pope seemed to have become almost a normal occurrence, in order to defuse, in a way that is necessary for survival, the conflict in which extremists of a wide variety of camps are trying to stir up billions of believers into an apocalyptic final battle against each other.

Here the Prince explicitly defended the Pope against those critics who were still trying to blame him for the Regensburg speech, and showed admiringly that it had become *de facto* an enormous catalyst of Christian-Muslim dialogue. Benedict XVI listened, nodded and smiled. For a moment he seemed to have forgotten all that lay ahead of him, for instance laying the foundation stone for two cathedrals on the Jordan River, at the deepest place on earth; from there he would set out for Jerusalem and then Golgotha.

But maybe he also thought back again for a moment to Mount Nebo, on which he had begun his pilgrim journey earlier with a view of the Promised Land, like John Paul II in the year 2000, and like Moses over 3,000 years ago. Carpets had been spread out for the Pope over the ruins of the old Byzantine Basilica of Moses. Jericho almost disappeared in the haze. The Dead Sea was a pool of gray in the depths. The grandiose view was completely concealed.

Yet the Holy Land is the Promised Land. It is larger, grounded in a tradition of longing "to see, to touch, and to savor in prayer and contemplation the places blessed by the physical presence of our Savior, His Blessed Mother, the apostles and the first disciples who saw Him risen from the dead." Desert birds whirled around the Pope as he looked over the railing toward the West. The wind billowed his cassock. "We know that, like Moses," he had said earlier, "we may not see the complete fulfillment of God's plan in our lifetime." Rain would have done the view some good. It was still milky around Jerusalem. Yet suddenly there was happiness on his face. Suddenly it was as though from Mount Nebo he could see all the way to the Heavenly Jerusalem.

Through the narrow gate—Jerusalem, May 11, 2009

In eternal Jerusalem the clocks still tick as always, maybe just a bit faster now with the arrival of the Pope from Germany. It is as tense as ever in the capital city of high tension. With the taxi drivers you have to haggle, now as before, over matters of course, and whether or not the meter should be on now. On the streets, horns mingle with screaming police sirens. The droning of the helicopters high above does not fade away. Security level 1+ rules during this supreme visit. Mohammed, the authority at the Damascus Gate, who has aged, by now no longer yearns for a third Intifada, but rather a terrible earthquake with which God should finally combine the mourning and weeping of both hostile peoples in this city into one single great lamentation, so that they might come together, first to convert and then to make peace. "God can do it! He can easily do it, and He will do it, too, when He has finally had enough of the lies!" But a new war and another and then another would never change anything here.

Maybe. Yet Jerusalem is more dazzling than ever in recent days. The May sun has brought the city's blossoms and flowers to the point of exploding all at once. Around Mount Herzl the blue of the rosemary has yielded to the yellow of the genista. Here — by the Yad Vashem Memorial, where Israel reminds the world that a crime against humanity at the hands of Germans was the ultimate reason for its emergence as a safe home for the Jewish people — stands the true and narrowest gate of this journey. Who could know that better than the Pope from Germany? Among the journalists from all over the world in his entourage, the argument of opinion makers about the appropriate interpretation begins very early in the hotel. After all, don't they have in their hands the new "disaster": the text of the speech — the next and last major misstep of the Pope with that strong German accent?

Nevertheless, as a prelude to his journey through the State of Israel, "the land that is so holy for so many millions of believers throughout the world," the pilgrim goes to Yad Vashem with a theology of the name into the Hall of Remembrance of the nameless terror. He relies on the faith-filled language of the Psalmist and on the author of Lamentations. Benedict XVI is poetic here in a way that is probably possible only after Auschwitz. At this place of the underworld the musical theologian comes once again not as a politician, not as a diplomat or a monarch, but rather in the role that is his favorite and most familiar: as a teacher of the Church. As an exegete he has always been at home. And so he is on his first day in Jerusalem, even now, at this place of the underworld.

Not one word about Pius XII, his predecessor, to whom in a Hall of Shame within the complex a photo with a questionable caption is dedicated, and also in many articles in the Israeli press in the previous days. At Ben Gurion Airport the Pope already made it clear that the "anti-Semitism" that "continues to rear its ugly head in many parts of the world … is totally unacceptable." Therefore "it is right and fitting that," in Israel, he should have "the opportunity to honor the memory of the six million Jewish victims" who had lost their lives as the terrible result of an ideology that denied the fundamental rights of the human person. At the airport he also took up the topic of Israel's conflict with the Palestinians and continued to speak about it in the residence of the President.

"Peace is above all a divine gift," he said there, and he quoted the Prophet Jeremiah: "I know the plans I have in mind for you—it is the Lord who speaks—plans for peace not disaster, to give you a future and a hope" (Jer. 29:11-12). It is absolutely necessary to discover these plans of God today. They can be found, however, only in a "united search for God"—and in listening together to his teachings. And in the correct interpretation, we can hear the former teacher saying in the background. He went on to say that "batah," the Hebrew term for security, which in such a special way dominates the entire reality of Israel, refers not just to the absence of a threat but is derived from the term trust. "Security, integrity, justice and peace" are inseparably related to one another according to God's plan.

Suddenly you could hear Martin Buber through the Pope's words. But then in Yad Vashem—the "Memorial of the Name"—it was almost exclusively Sacred Scripture itself with which the first Catholic addressed the descendants of the victims among the "countless descendants of Abraham." "One can rob a neighbor of possessions, opportunity or freedom. One can weave an insidious web of lies to convince others that certain groups are undeserving of respect. Yet, try as one might, one can never take away the *name* of a fellow human being." Those who died in the *Shoah* lost their lives, but they could never lose their names. Here, in Yad Vashem, they are therefore gathered forever, for eternity, in the memory of the almighty God of Abraham, Isaac and Jacob, to whom Jesus addressed His prayers.

The flame flickers gently in front of the old man in white, who is reminiscent here of the younger but much frailer John Paul II, who nine years ago wheezed here in such a way that one could fear for his life and breath. Benedict XVI seems much more delicate and vulnerable in this hall than his predecessor, and also wounded. He did not come as a hero to this land, where Hebrew announcers in an endless loop belabor their commentaries on the ceremony again and again with the German word *Wehrmacht* [armed forces, in which Joseph Ratzinger did compulsory service in 1943-1945]. Only in meetings with elderly survivors who are introduced to him does a smile flit over his face, and his eyebrows become animated.

He intended to come to Jerusalem as a Roman, and yet he stands there as a German again. His English suddenly becomes even more German than before. He came as a priest and yet is called to account over and over for the crimes of the Nazis. His eyelashes quiver as he looks at the flame, his hands seek each other like sibling children who could get lost in the dark as he listens to the fates of the victims, which are recited in the presence of the President, the rabbis, the guests and listeners all over the globe. His lips move imperceptibly. The cries of the murdered children, whose parents had such great hopes for them, are an echo of the cry of murdered Abel, the victim of the first fratricide, the Pope says, before he relies at the conclusion, exhausted and sorrowful, on the hope of the Jewish Lamentations: "The favors of the Lord are not exhausted, His mercies are not spent; They are renewed each morning, so great is His faithfulness."

At the world's navel—Jerusalem, May 12, 2009

As-salámu 'aláikum! Many in the Levant had been waiting for this Arabic greeting, but the Pope saved it for his visit to the Grand Mufti in the Dome of the Rock, at the place which in Judaism is regarded by many as the navel of the world, because here God Himself abolished human sacrifice forever through the example of the patriarch Abraham. Isaac, Abraham's son, was the first victim who no longer had to die, but rather—on the contrary—became the father of all Jews. Benedict XVI does not fulfill any expectations (however strong the pressure may be in the fiery furnace of this pilgrim journey), but he surpasses them again and again.

The sun was reflected in the gold of the cupola. The Pope removed his shoes. In the streets of Jerusalem pilgrims often move as though in church. But if there really is holy ground in this city—like in the wilderness in front of the burning bush, where God Himself commanded Moses to take off his sandals—then it is here. The ground of the Dome of the Rock is thrice holy, for Jews, Muslims, and Christians, and therefore exponentially more susceptible to conflict.

Minutes later the Pope stood at the Wailing Wall, at the foot of the Temple Mount that is crowned by the Dome of the Rock. It had become hot. A dove had landed in a caper bush on the gigantic wall over the little man in white. Two swallows swooped down on him, chirping in the silence. The wind lifted his white mozetta, as if he himself might learn once again to fly after all. The gold cross on his chest gleamed in the sun.

Jesus had seen this wall, the Pope knows. Mary, His Mother, had heard the knocking of the stonemasons in her childhood in front of the door of her parents' house. The wall is a stone mirror of the ages. God looks through the cracks in the wall at His people who have returned, many believe. And this is certain: the Wailing Wall is a retaining wall of Israel's history on its journey through time.

Motionless, Benedict looks at the stones. After a Hebrew psalm, he recites Psalm 122 in Latin in a firm voice:

> I was glad when they said to me, "Let us go to
>   the house of the LORD!"
> Our feet have been standing within your gates,
>   O Jerusalem! ...
> May they prosper who love you! ...
> For my brethren and companions' sake I will
>   say, "Peace be within you!"
> For the sake of the house of the LORD our God, I
>   will seek your good.

It is the psalm of all pilgrims to Jerusalem. John Paul II had already prayed it here — although Benedict XVI never imitates him, not even with his message on a piece of paper that he slips into a crack in the wall, like countless pilgrims before him. It reads: "God of all the ages, on my visit to Jerusalem, the 'City of Peace,' spiritual home to Jews, Christians and Muslims alike, I bring before You the joys, the hopes and the aspirations, the trials, the suffering and the pain of all Your people throughout the world. God of Abraham, Isaac and Jacob, hear the cry of the afflicted, the fearful, the bereft; send Your peace upon this Holy Land, upon the Middle East, upon the entire human family; stir the hearts of all who call upon Your name, to walk humbly in the path of justice and compassion. 'The Lord is good to those who wait for Him, to the soul that seeks Him!'"

Silently he stands in front of the wall afterward, upright. He is praying, of course. He bows slightly. Turns around—and sets out for the origin of Christendom, the Cenacle on Mount Zion, through the Valley of Josaphat, where Jesus once wept over Jerusalem, at the place of Judaism's Last Judgment between the Mount of Olives and the Temple Mount, to strengthen the Christians of the city in their "battle of hope against despair, frustration and cynicism." Actually Benedict XVI doesn't have a chance here, yet he does the best he can with the opportunity.

Radical partisanship—Jerusalem, May 14, 2009

If Pope Benedict XVI, on his trip to Amman after Jerusalem, had taken the Mercedes and not the airplane, he would have seen something that any pilgrim here can grasp with his hands and feet. Israel's new highway from the Jordan to Jerusalem—diagonally through the West Bank!—defies any political intention ever to give this region back to the Palestinians for their own state. No one will bet even a shekel on such a state in the future. Are things that belong together therefore growing together here now as well? Yes and no. It is true that the Holy Land has a profound unity. It is also true that there are various owners of the land, whose claims and titles to ownership are diametrically contradictory. That makes the conflict in many respects hopeless within the East-West "clash of civilizations"—and unfortunately it also makes more comprehensible the frenzy of security into which Israel increasingly falls.

How does it happen, then, that the eighty-two-year-old Pope, after his strenuous pilgrim journey through the heart of this agitated region of crisis, is nevertheless returning to Rome now so rested, relaxed and, indeed, happy? Had he not had a down payment of agitation in Europe in recent months? He worked no miracle in the Holy Land. However, He did accomplish there one feat that is not always kindly regarded. For there, at every step of his pilgrim journey, he was radically partisan—but for both sides! Above all, though, he was and persistently remains a partisan of rational forgiveness in the midst of the tragedy of all the traumas that hold the peoples of the Holy Land prisoner in many ways. Who can expect that he will only make friends thereby—or reap only applause? Yet already in Jordan, with this course of action, the Pope opened up and extended the circle of rational actors in a new East-West Divan [allusion to an anthology of poems by Goethe] among billions of Muslims and Christians, who must not let themselves be baited into a holy war, if only for the sake of the continued existence of the planet. Anyone can read the speeches from the trip. Yet eight years after the burning Twin Towers and three years after Regensburg, Benedict XVI has now staged a change of images in the Holy Land too—where in front of the cameras of the Arabic network Al Jazeera the successor of Peter visits the tall descendant of the Prophet in his mosque and the Pope listens to Prince Ghazi bin Muhammad bin Talal as though on a medieval miniature, in which a crusader leans peacefully over a game of chess with Saladin, the "noble knight" of the Levant, in an almost forgotten vision of peace.

But of course Benedict XVI is not a crusader. Therefore the attentively listening Pope makes a more lasting impression as he powerfully and gently works for a union of reason against all the forms of totalitarianism with which the modern era has already benefited humanity. He does not have to be loud. He embodies a tradition that has no peer anywhere in the world. In Amman

Prince Ghazi even congratulated him on his liberalization of the Tridentine Rite, because Muslims apparently have observed better than many Catholics that the Catholic Church thereby became more capable of dialogue with other religions whose roots similarly mean a lot to them. The images of the Pope's silence in front of Jerusalem's Wailing Wall and his lament in front of the barricade around Bethlehem will last.

Yet even more moving will be the memory of him standing so helplessly in front of the eternal flame at Vad Yashem. Blinking nervously. Where what anyone says can never be enough. And so at first he did not try at all. The curse of the evil deed weighs heavily on the room. Neither does the Pope let himself be forced, though, into the role of an agent of injustice or an acolyte of hell. He just stood there; that was all that he could do. The only thing anyone can honestly do here—where he then hesitantly, shyly sputtered while intoning a song in praise of God's name and recalled God as a living being in the presence of the incomprehensible horror of death. "I know that my redeemer lives!" he whispered with unfortunate Job. Here the past will never fade away—here the pilgrim from Rome, with every step he took, exhorted mankind to make a lasting peace with the future, and with eternity.

Condoms, Cases of Sexual Abuse, and a Liturgical Work of Art in the United Kingdom — 2010

The Rock from the day before yester-yesterday: A plea —
Rome, January 29, 2010

We are not Pope and never were, thank God: neither the author of these lines nor Klaus Wowereit [politician] nor Dieter Bohlen [pop singer] nor any other German — and a good thing, too. Not even Angela Merkel and Margot Kässmann [Lutheran bishop] were ever Pope, and certainly not all of us Germans together. The slogan that once maintained the contrary was a clever tabloid headline, but still an idiotic wink from the wit factory of the Frankfurt School. We have not been Frenchmen either since Joseph Cardinal Ratzinger was elected to the Académie Française in 1992.

Of course neither was Alexander Smoltczyk's elegant observation in *Der Spiegel* that the Germans in April 2005 "lost their faith in godlessness" ever true. That sense was due only to the overwhelming experience of those days on Saint Peter's Square, when even religiously tone-deaf people thought that they heard again something of the choir of angels in the last Pope's death rattle. With the election of Benedict XVI, others were overwhelmed by the deceptive assumption that the great world war of the nations had thereby finally come to an end. Today this euphoria is spent. Now the godless are making their presence felt again, more doggedly than ever before in my lifetime, and as aggressively as if they were intent on winning back lost territory.

Clearly Benedict XVI has automatically come into the crosshairs of their heavy artillery. After all, he offers no resistance. He does not defend himself. He will not make the rounds of the talk shows. But nobody more maddeningly stands in the path of the furor of the failed leftist social engineers of yesterday. By now quite a few of them have been earning their living as the language policemen of a new civil religion that worships everything (except God) that serves man's self-empowerment over life and death and destiny. Among them the good old agitprop is now positioned against the last bastion that still resists this project: Church and Pope.

For Roman observers, however, it still seems strange, how silently so many brave heroes in Germany duck when the defamatory, demagogical accusations are hurled. In this regard even the Bishops' Conference falls into an anxious, frightened stupor—and it allows its news agency to feed once again to every editor between Aachen and Passau the dreadful report about what Joseph Alois Ratzinger's great-uncle (!) in the nineteenth century (!!) allegedly said about the Jews, in a sort of journalistic guilt by association going back three generations. Not one word of indignation about that from Berlin.

In Italy almost every relevant word of the Pope provides for vigorous debates in the newspapers, from left to right. Through their identification with the Pope, the Poles brought on the collapse of the Soviet system from Berlin to the Bering Strait. The worst accusation from Germany against Pope Benedict XVI, though, after analyzing all the arguments, is really that he is a German (and therefore of course also a dyed-in-the-wool anti-Semite, etc., etc.). It goes without saying that Englishmen would raise this subject immediately after the election. But many observers in Rome, Warsaw, or Paris can only rub their eyes in astonishment over the fact that this accusation is now being aired in the land of the Reformation itself.

Yes, in Germany everything is permitted, except one thing: showing solidarity with the Pope. He is the most modern Pontiff there has ever been, his keen mind and erudition are world-famous, his doctrine of the separation of Church and State is radical, he is a Buddha on the Chair of Peter, he is the most Jewish pope since the early days of Christianity, he is the most ecumenical one that we may ever have (although he does not favor abolishing all trade barriers), even though many people will not realize that—if they ever do—until the next pope is elected from China or Brazil. Yet he is a German. Oh, nooooo! This is why it is necessary to speak here briefly about his faith.

Catholics not only believe in one God, but as a consequence of this conviction, they also believe that truth exists. That means one truth, and not two, three, four, or countless truths. And what is true cannot at the same time be untrue; even audacious repetitions do not make falsehoods true. Pious Catholics, moreover, share this faith in the existence of one truth with pious Jews and pious Muslims, and thanks to religious liberty no one today is forced to subscribe to the Catholic Creed. For in our part of the world, this belief in the truth in the modern era was professed by the great Catholic Alexis de Tocqueville (a contemporary of Karl Marx), when he acknowledged: "I think that I would have loved freedom in all eras. In the era in which we live, however, I feel inclined to worship it."

Nevertheless, Her rigid dealings with the truth continue to make the Catholic Church a bit inflexible toward all those who have and advocate one opinion today and another tomorrow, because in their view there is no universally valid truth. Nothing but haunting spirits of the times. And they haunt along with them. Yesterday a Communist, today an apocalyptic, tomorrow a Buddhist, the day after tomorrow maybe a moon-worshipper. And somehow that is human, too: all-too-human. Less human, however, is the inquisitorial furor with which they step on the gas at every new bend and curve.

I do not have to explain that there are two incompatible worlds confronting each other here. Whereas believers lean on the truth (even if it is still partially hidden) as a deeply anchored mode of being, genuine atheists lack this stationary pole. Ultimately there is nothing that they can lean on, because nothing is reliably consistent. They would like to be on the right side for once, finally. This is what drives them, and this has its dangers.

And this is what Joseph Cardinal Ratzinger meant on the eve of his election to the papacy when he warned about a menacing "dictatorship of relativism." For someone who tries to flatten the difference between truth and falsehood will try to flatten other distinctions too. Why not? You can say anything, after all. Everything is relative. There is no truth. There are only those who claim that it exists. That's why Benedict XVI bothers some people; that's why they lump him in with the Taliban. Be that as it may. But yesterday I had to read that the man from Bavaria is not only German but also "from the day before yesterday," and then it definitely became ridiculous. After all, he is not a man from the day before yesterday. He is from yester-yester-yester-yesterday.

He is two thousand years old. He is Peter. He is a Galilean and comes from Bethsaida on the sea. That is why he so radically reconciles the Catholic Church with Her authentic, apostolic and (despite all breaks) ultimately unbroken Tradition, back to Her origin in Jesus of Nazareth, who said of Himself: "I am the way, and the truth, and the life" (John 14:6).

Someone who does not understand this has understood nothing about the Catholic Church. Benedict XVI has pledged himself body and soul to the eternal Truth of the merciful God, for whom he will also die like his predecessor. He is a man of the day before yester-yesterday and of two days after tomorrow. How many empires have crumbled in the last two thousand years? The Pope remains.

Hosanna, hosanna — Rome, March 28, 2010

This year Palm Sunday could not have begun more beautifully. Jubilant blackbirds in the dark of the night. After that a cloudless spring morning. The granite block of the obelisk on Saint Peter's Square wreathed with fresh flowers. Laurel with white buttercups, hydrangeas, gillyflowers. Next to it an olive tree, an upright alabaster crucifix, the keys and the crown as papal insignia, not made of gold, but woven out of bleached palm leaves, on which the morning sun played.

The week before, the successor of Peter had suffered as seldom before in his pontificate. In Germany a barrage of stories tried to drag him by force into the mud-wrestling match over cases of sexual abuse from decades ago, which had been made public in the previous weeks. In Munich teams from American networks were under way, turning over every stone in order to involve him personally in the case of a priest who had become too intrusive in the 1980's. Money was no object for the desired mega-scoop. The Pope had to be caught. In Regensburg others tried to wrap his older brother Georg in the mantle of a punishing pedagogue, several days after he had already apologized for "*Watschn*" [boxes on the ear] that he had dealt thirty years before. No end to the hunt was in sight as the Palm Sunday procession stepped onto Saint Peter's Square, representing Jesus' triumphal entrance into Jerusalem—before he was lifted up as King of the Jews on the Cross.

In the lead were acolytes with the Crucifix, behind them the choir, and next countless priests, bishops in violet and cardinals in scarlet, all with palm branches. A walking forest. Gregorian chants wafting over them. And below them and behind them, bent over, as though he were the weakest of all, finally Peter, in his royal cope. In Christ's purple garments he concluded this triumphant procession instead of the king of mockery, being the "Servant of the servants of God," as Rome's bishops have been called since Gregory the Great. A woven palm scepter in his hand, the epitome of powerlessness. So he listens in front of the obelisk to the Scriptural readings for that Sunday, behind a curtain of incense that rises to heaven from the sacred books like a prayer. Behind him nothing but the base of the obelisk. Only the rock wall in which stone-masons centuries ago hammered the Church's victorious song:

> CHRISTVS VINCIT
> CHRISTVS REGNAT
> CHRISTVS IMPERAT
> CHRISTVS AB OMNI MALO
> PLEBEM SVAM
> DEFENDAT

Christ conquers.
Christ reigns.
Christ rules.
May Christ defend His people against all evil.

Yet the Pontiff's silence is mightier, as a vocabulary word from God's language of gestures. The image becomes disturbingly eloquent as the deacon steps to the lectern and chants to the unmoved Pope the song of the Suffering Servant of God, in which the Prophet Isaiah already captured, centuries before the first Palm Sunday, *how* God wants to conquer in Christ, to rule and defend His people from all evil:

> The Lord GOD has opened my ear,
> and I was not rebellious,
> I turned not backward.
> I gave my back to those who struck me,
> and my cheeks to those who pulled out the beard;
> I hid not my face
> from shame and spitting.
> For the Lord GOD helps me;
> therefore I have not been confounded;
> therefore I have set my face like a flint,
> and I know that I shall not be put to
> shame. (Isa. 50:5-7)

On the bridge of a leaking boat—Rome, April 15, 2010

It was pouring rain on Easter morning as Pope Benedict XVI sprinkled the altar on Saint Peter's Square with holy water from a silver bucket. Wasn't it absurd? Wasn't everything already wet enough? Did he not see the umbrellas, as far as the eye could see? Yes, and it was an unusually fine metaphor for how the world of the Catholic liturgy is becoming increasingly estranged from the world of media perception. It was a real "clash of civilizations" in which the collision of different cultures threatens to tear the Catholic Church apart from within. Every day new statistics about those leaving the Church are reported, especially in Germany, where more and more people have long since relied on the daily news than on the "Good News" of the Gospel. And so it may have seemed nothing short of incomprehensible to many that the Pope on Easter said not one word about the cases of pedophile abuse that have been preoccupying the media in the Western world in wave after wave — and which he had addressed several days previously with a long letter to the Irish. On Easter the Pope does not preside over a press conference, but rather the celebration of the Resurrection of Jesus Christ from the dead. In that hour he addressed 1.2 billion Catholics in a message from Rome — "*urbi et orbi*" [to the city and to the world]. For as Benedict XVI, Joseph Ratzinger is no longer a German, even though he now challenges his former compatriots — and many Swiss — as no man has done since Martin Luther. That never was his ambition. He would have preferred to return quietly to his old home. He would have wished even more to be able to complete his book about Jesus of Nazareth in complete peace, when on April 19, 2005 — three days after his seventy-eighth birthday five years ago! — he suddenly became the 264th successor of the Apostle Peter and as head of the worldwide Catholic Church was catapulted into the blinding glare of the spotlights. There was no career strategy behind it. Terrible fear gripped him during the election. Several days afterward he still spoke about the blade of the guillotine that he saw rushing down at him as the cardinals voted. For he had no illusions about the condition of the Catholic Church.

"Lord, your Church often seems like a boat about to sink, a boat taking in water on every side," he had exclaimed eight days before the death of John Paul II in front of the Colosseum in an urgent prayer over a sea of flickering candles. "The soiled garments and face of your Church throw us into confusion. Yet it is we ourselves who have soiled them! It is we who betray you time and time again, after all our lofty words and grand gestures.... When we fall, we drag you down to earth, and Satan laughs, for he hopes that you will not be able to rise from that fall; he hopes that being dragged down in the fall of your Church, you will remain prostrate and overpowered." His analysis could have been no more unsparing yesterday, after the five years that he has now already stood on the bridge of the boat, which seems to be "taking in water on every side." In his lifetime the waves have never surged higher. One tsunami after another is shaking the two-thousand-year-old ship from stem to stern. The mast is hacked to pieces; the planks groan.

And what is the captain of Peter's ship doing? Has he perhaps fallen asleep? Is he dreaming? In a certain way, yes. In fact he is still pursuing his old dream: with his last strength and for heaven's sake to come to a happy end with his book about Jesus of Nazareth! To testify credibly once again for the beginning of the new millennium to the Incarnation of God in Jesus Christ (in Mary) and His Resurrection from the dead. Why is he doing that? Is it his desire to think, his desire to formulate, his desire to write that so many hold against him, whereas they think that he ought to rule at last, abolish celibacy, introduce women priests and "gender mainstreaming," allow condoms and abortion and in general abolish the papacy at a new Council? Instead, in an extremely irritating way, in the midst of all these storms, he picks up his pencil every minute that he can spare for it and continues to write his book, as his mother once took up her knitting to make warm sweaters for him and his brother.

Perhaps therefore this is a proof of heavenly humor: that the cardinals elected him, of all people, to steer the ship of the Church through the first storms of the digital revolution, through dangers that no pope before him could imagine. It has been his lot, in any case, to become the first pope in the age of headlong acceleration—in which we can already say goodbye to every abbey with an internet connection in its cloistered cells that suddenly enables the monks, who before had voluntarily withdrawn from the world, to surf on the World Wide Web without restrictions or limits. A 1,500-year-old culture is coming to an end before our eyes. Like no one else he is familiar with such ruptures, but also with all the failure, all the sin and all the crimes within the Church. All the more puzzling, therefore, is the unfailing composure with which he refuses to let himself be driven by public opinion. He has no lack of real enemies, in New York and Beijing as well as in the halls of the Vatican, who have many different motives. He opposes all the advocates of collective guilt. He has never signed on to faddish multiculturalism. In the minefield of the Near East he is consistent and never stops recommending a two-state solution. In America, with his rigorous teachings on ethical questions he stands in the way of the bioengineers—and the billion-dollar business that beckons behind them. There are plenty of reasons, then, for trying to delegitimize the papacy and for deconstructing the Catholic Church's authority in moral, political and ethical questions.

For this reason, too, the Pope continues to devote every free minute to his book. That may sound absurd and yet it is strictly logical. For behind all the crises Benedict sees that he is confronted during his papacy with a much more dramatic catastrophe than the one that everybody is talking about now. It is the collapse of the faith within one generation. This is no longer a matter of a scandal here and a scandalous interview there. It is about the heart of the faith: about Jesus Christ. Less than thirty percent of the people in Germany still believe in eternal life—and among them are a series of prominent theologians. Probably even fewer believe in Christ's Resurrection. The comment boxes of the new online media are overflowing with a groundswell of aggression against the Church. For this reason too, Benedict XVI would like best to keep writing his book, even on his eighty-third birthday. He celebrates his name days: Joseph on March 19, Benedict on July 11. Nevertheless, his birthday today will certainly turn his attention again to his parents, whose faith and honor he wants to salvage in his book: the "faith of our fathers," as it used to be called.

This look back at parents is the key to and epitome of all tradition. It is the two-thousand-year-old faith of the Church which he intends now as the Pope and the leading theologian of our time to defend once more against all those colleagues in his guild who thought that they had to reinvent the faith. Therefore last year he proclaimed a "Year of the Priest" for an absolutely necessary purification of the Catholic elite. Therefore he undertook the daring adventure of reconciliation with the Society of Saint Pius X. This is a radical re-commissioning of the Church with the latest arguments concerning Tradition as a whole, and the enormous task haunts him. That is why he is staking his life on a retelling of the story of Jesus of Nazareth, in whom God assumed His unmistakable human face.

Benedict Up Close

In the cockpit — Castel Gandolfo, Summer 2010

During his vacation, the Pope's view from his office looks to the East over Lake Albano, to the West toward the sea and to the North toward Rome, where on clear days he can make out the dome of Saint Peter's Cathedral in the distance. It is a panoramic view, as though from the cockpit of an airplane, yet most of all he likes to lower his glance to the white sheet of paper in front of him, on which he so urgently wants to complete Part Three of his Jesus trilogy. Therefore Benedict XVI already decided a year ago not to spend summer in the high mountains, which he loves, but instead to set out for the Alban Hills directly from Rome. Castel Gandolfo has an ideal elevation, an atmosphere where he knows his way around with his eyes shut and is in rest-and-recreation mode from the very first day, without acclimatization phases and the enormous security apparatus that otherwise would have to be set into motion again. At the age of eighty-three he now sets other priorities even when on vacation. He broke his left hand at the beginning of his vacation in the Aosta Valley three years ago and took it as a warning signal.

His daily routine is a little more relaxed, his spiritual life unabridged, his breakfast identical — a German-Italian combination that has its sweet biscotti and croissant-shaped cornetti too — and there is no change of menu at the other meals. Italy's recipes are in keeping with his native fondness for flour-based dishes, and the rest is determined by the seasons in the farms around Castel Gandolfo; only on Sunday evenings is there bread with cold cuts as formerly in Bavaria. If no extra guests are present in the family of his little living community, mealtime at midday lasts forty-five minutes, and in the evening — a half hour. Even during vacation, gluttony is as foreign to him as *Schnaps* [liquor] or gymnastics in front of an open window. His sensual pleasures are of another sort.

Just having a little more time is for him a great pleasure. Being able to extend slightly a block of his personal time. Being able to read for a short time undisturbed is a luxury for him: now the biography of one of his contemporaries or a classic novel that he always wanted to read someday, or having time for his older brother Georg, who always comes to visit him for a few weeks at the beginning of the vacation. For after all, even as Pope he has remained what he always was: a very methodical man—if possible without surprises and interruptions, which of course on most days even during vacation can only be a pious wish. Letters continue to flow unimpeded via many pipelines into the summer residence, with the usual urgent inquiries.

Therefore, more than any holiday, what he likes most about these days is a rhythm without interruptions, in which he can resume work on his book according to a definite schedule, as often as possible. What the swimming pool was for John Paul II in his younger years, creative work still is for Benedict XVI, who now is already older than his predecessor ever was. Whatever he needs from any books for the necessary scholarly background research, the last pope of the Gutenberg era has filed as neatly in his head as any computer could have done. Before he sits down at his writing desk, he has his private secretary set up a little apparatus with the scholarly works that he will consult. No hidden door leads from his office to the information highways of the virtual world. It goes without saying that he has no personal computer here and no internet connection, but only the white paper and the pencil in front of him, in one of the last oases in the digital cosmos. He glides in thought like an eagle back and forth through the high mountains of his knowledge and experiences before setting the words to paper, even today using techniques just as analog as those of Saint Jerome in his study. Vacation? For the old priest it must be a bit of heaven already to draw close to Jesus once again as an intellectual over this paper.

At quarter to seven sharp, though, the pencil rests. Then Our Lady waits for him in the garden, and he comes to her as punctually as guests of state to one of his audiences. The chirping of birds accompanies him and his secretary on the shady rosary path. No mobile phone, nothing at all can disturb him here among the mossy old trees. By now he walks slightly bent over and uses a cane on the path of his predecessors, whose prayers he continues to recite here. He is at home here. Vacation? There is the bench by the fish pond at the end of the path, where he rests in front of the picture of Mary like Joseph in Nazareth, to whose Son he has signed over his life.

Holy Grandfather — London, September 27, 2010

"No," the Pope said already on board the *Città di Fiumincino*, on the way to Edinburgh, in response to the question: Should the Church urgently reconsider how She can be made more attractive again? "Anyone who asks how the Church can be made more attractive has lost his way and gone astray with the question itself." The Church is not selling anything, least of all Herself, but rather Good News has been entrusted to Her, and She must hand it on in its entirety. Benedict XVI seemed hoarse. His eyes sparkled, but at the end of the little press conference above the clouds, when he turned around, the eighty-three-year-old Pontiff walked back to his seat as bent over as though the burden of his officer were crushing him even before the start of his trip to visit the Britons. Soon after had he landed, though, he stood upright and seemed stronger from one hour to the next.

After that he made the Catholic Church with Her undiluted message as attractive as it perhaps has ever been since the days of the first missionaries to the uncouth Anglo-Saxons, yet without any discount in matters of faith and truth and without skipping any "dogma," as John Henry Newman would have said. He condemned the "unspeakable crimes" of pathological abuse more clearly than ever. Nevertheless, that was not his reason for coming to England—and he soon made that much clearer still. Quietly, modestly, and cheerfully he proclaimed anew the Gospel of Christ, constantly varying the message—in the age of a rampant alienation of society as a whole from its Christian roots. After three days, the *Sunday Times* corrected the English image of Pope Ratzinger with the words: "Rottweiler? No, he is the Holy Grandfather." It was the complete transformation of a five-year-old public image, and a troop of journalists watched in astonishment: "Britain learnt to love the Pope."

In the dusk, as the bells of Westminster Abbey sounded the tocsin above the jubilant crowd of people in the heart of London Town at his departure, he had not only won back his own perennial themes and the hearts of millions, but also the approval of an overwhelming majority of the media. He had surprised them already in Edinburgh in the Queen's presence: with a key speech about "the sobering lessons" taught by "the world's atheistic extremism in the twentieth century." When he spoke in Westminster Hall to the Elite of British society, one could have heard a pin drop. It was the same room in which the Lord Chancellor Thomas More had been condemned to death in the year 1535. This was no pop "magical mystery tour"; it was living history when the Pope praised this Catholic martyr, right there, as a crown witness of the sovereignty of conscience, "which he followed..., even at the cost of displeasing the sovereign whose 'good servant' he was." What the Pope gave the proud Britons here was a lecture on the fundamental pillars of democracy; he went so far as to defend the Christmas holiday on the civil calendar. Until his final breath he will resist the marginalization of religion in the public arena. And until then, in any case, he will keep fine-tuning the keynote of his pontificate: the dialogue and exchange between faith and reason, which is indispensable for everyone if mankind cares about its future.

Here he is in agreement with Rowan Williams, the Archbishop of Canterbury, whom he embraces more cordially than almost anyone else on this journey. After an ecumenical vespers service (and celestial singing) in Westminster Abbey, he let the chief Anglican lead him down the steps on his arm, like a friend, after having reminded him of his predecessor Gregory the Great, who once coined the description of the popes as "Servants of the servants of God," and of Benedict the Great [the founder of Western monasticism], whose vision for the West the Pope takes up again today, so as to let the beauty and the splendor that was first "revealed in the Face of Jesus Christ" shine anew upon the world.

It was perhaps the finest response to the intellectual and liturgical multi-media artwork of this journey. It was stirring. From that moment on — at latest — the two men have been going further ahead on a path that no one before them had trod. It has long since seemed that Benedict XVI arrived in England not by plane and popemobile but rather on the shoulders of John Henry Newman, the prophetic giant of intellect and faith, whose works he catapulted into the middle of the Church during these days. Now, though, because he sits on his shoulders, he looms over him also in his view of the horizons of the modern world.

In Birmingham he reminded the bishops of the United Kingdom that "if we are to be effective Christian leaders, we must live lives of the utmost integrity, humility and holiness." John Henry Newman wrote: "O that God would grant the clergy to feel their weakness as sinful men, and the people to sympathize with them and love them and pray for their increase in all good gifts of grace." So he too prays that Christian leaders will dedicate themselves more intensely to their prophetic vocation and sanctification. "Prayer for vocations will then arise spontaneously, and we may be confident that the Lord will respond by sending labourers to bring in the plentiful harvest that he has prepared throughout the United Kingdom." God created everyone for a very particular task, he says, recalling Newman's insight: "He has committed some work to me which He has not committed to another."

Even before that he had recalled again and again in various ways Newman's radical rejection of any relative arbitrariness, and emphasized that for the Church there can be no "middle path" in a world of many "truths" that are supposedly equally valid. In reunited Germany, however, this is viewed quite differently; upon his return he had to read news reports about Thomas von Mitschke-Collande, who recently urged the German Bishops' Conference to discuss at their next meeting questions such as the revision and justification of the exercise of intra-ecclesial authority, "communion for the remarried, sexual morality, the role of women and [equal] access to the priesthood." These debates must not be understood as an attack, the business consultant from Tutzing insisted, but should be regarded as the working of the Holy Spirit. In short, in Her "profound identity crisis" the

Church, which is anxiously overlooking her opportunities, must again courageously become "capable of campaigning."

That is true: the Church really does need courage, particularly in Germany. She is in big trouble. (Who could doubt it?) She lies sick in bed. But only someone who wishes Her dead can suggest listening in this condition to business consultants and other professionals from the advertising industry instead of to Pope Benedict XVI, Blessed John Henry Newman and other saints who faced death courageously—or even just to the Silesian Baroque poet Friedrich von Logau (1605-1655), who back at the time of the Thirty Years' War recognized: "In danger and great need, / the middle path brings death."

Prophylactics instead of pro-fidelity—Rome, November 25, 2010

Why are we getting excited about a subordinate clause about condoms in the Pope's new book, for which he again met with Peter Seewald for several interviews? At a decisive moment hardly anyone is going to cite the Church's prohibitions. Nor does it take the problem of AIDS off the table. Even the Pope is not that almighty.

Sexual relations are always "safest" with one's own husband or one's own wife—insofar as both are faithful. By and large, if I have not misinterpreted anything, this is what the Catholic Church teaches and what the popes have maintained for decades with astonishing stubbornness against an increasingly predominant lobby of condom police, who already tried to issue an international arrest warrant for Benedict XVI because in March 2009 on his flight to Cameroon he had dared to say "that the problem of AIDS cannot be solved with advertising slogans alone or by the distribution of prophylactics."

As a matter of public health, this view is reasonable, as statistics in Africa show, for example. In Swaziland (with 5 percent of its population Catholic), 43 percent are infected with AIDS, while in Uganda (with Catholics at 36 percent), only 4 percent are. In Washington, D.C., where condoms are distributed for free, the rate of infection has by now become higher than in West Africa. That is a preliminary observation. Next, it can hardly be called realistic to think that a Catholic man or woman who has just committed adultery and/or gone to a brothel would suddenly say at the decisive moment, "No, thank you, no condom. I'm Catholic." Or what African on the Dark Continent might reflect at the decisive moment and say: "What, a condom? For heaven's sake, no! The Pope has forbidden it, after all."

This notion is simply crazy. Any man and any woman who wants to will use condoms. No pope can forbid it. The combined forces of his Swiss Guard can do nothing about it. Even Pope Benedict XVI recalled this again, when in his book-length interview with Peter Seewald—on pages 118-119—he happened to speak about this obvious fact. With well-rehearsed, sincerely felt horror or delight, nevertheless, the entire media world again pounced first on this incidental remark the moment it was made public. At the press conference in which the exciting interview book was presented to the world public, there was a crowd the likes of which has not been seen since the death of John Paul II. The great majority of the questions, however, still concentrated on the little rubber prophylactic, until finally Peter Seewald himself spoke up. It is true, he said, the Catholic Church is in a major crisis. Everyone knows that now. Society, too, is in a crisis. Who is unaware of that? Now, though, we must finally speak also about a crisis of journalism, when the world is on the brink of the abyss, and the Pope as never before informs us about it—and his colleagues nevertheless still ask him again what he thinks about condoms. To that we can add only the book itself. It is entitled *Light of the World* and is now available in any bookstore. But best of all, in pharmacies too.

Ecumenism and Eclipse of God
in Germany — 2011

Fear not the Man in White — Rome, September 20, 2011
Benedict XVI comes back to Germany tomorrow as a *"homo historicus"* [historical man] *par excellence*. Without a look back at history, today's perception of the Pope in his homeland is barely intelligible. For one thing, Germany is not Poland. Poland remained united even when the country no longer existed at all, for centuries. The Poles did not lose their identity while under the tsars and the Prussians, not even under the Nazis or the Bolsheviks. Germany, on the other hand, remained divided, even during its most adventurous projects toward unification. The Germans, in the heart of Europe, with the most neighbors at their borders, have for centuries been preoccupied with the same question — who they really are, where they came from, and where they are going. This will-o'-the-wisp deep in the German soul led a good sixth of our elected representatives to take to their heels last Thursday when the little man in white was about to give a speech in the Parliament on the Jewish-Christian roots of Europe. This weakness of identity shared by

the parliamentarians has various roots. The Germans understood their first state—under Charlemagne, beginning 1200 years ago, in Aachen!—not as something German, but as a "Roman Empire." The conflict with the popes finally resulted in a "Holy Roman Empire" under Barbarossa, but only centuries later was the phrase "of the German Nation" added as a postscript. Since the eleventh century, however, almost every generation in Germany has observed a "Ditch Rome" movement, which in 1517 achieved its goal for the first time with the Reformation, unfortunately at the cost of splitting the Church apart, even if the first Protestants were not aware of it.

A man like Calvin, for instance, to his dying day, still quite naturally claimed to be "Catholic." There was the one great, right-believing Church—what else was there—in which there was just this damned conflict with the stubborn "Papists," at whom progressive "Catholics" of that era like Calvin or Melanchthon looked askance, despising them as perhaps today Hans Küng still despises the Society of Saint Pius X. The story did not stop there. Martin Luther himself would for this reason probably feel more at home today and get along better with the same Society than in a typical Protestant congregation in Hanover—while the overwhelming majority of German Catholics are by now in many respects much more Protestant than Luther ever was in his lifetime.

But that cannot be said at all by Benedict XVI here and now. He may have trouble with English pronunciation. His French is brilliant—like his Latin, Italian, German, ancient Greek, and Bavarian dialect. But above all he has a command of, speaks, and understands—as few others these days—"Catholic." He embodies an identity that, in Europe, leaves any national dimension far behind. No wonder he finds himself on a collision course with many a hothead in Germany. For in his homeland, the Pope comes not only to the Catholics, but also very deliberately to all Germans; to the old center of divided Christendom, therefore, which in many respects has become fossilized in this land of the Reformation—even though Catholics here, like Protestants, often can hardly explain the difference that separates them in faith, even in interdenominational marriages.

Furthermore the old fronts in the religious wars have long since taken a new course. Here it is no longer the Catholics and the Protestants who stand in opposition to one another. In the East, after two dictatorships on German soil, only a very few of them have remained, making way for a complacent majority of nihilists and neo-pagans. The Catholics cannot get over the trauma of their old division, and are constantly playing out little epilogues to the Reformation in various camps. Meanwhile, in the East as in the West, all Christians are now beset by a new civil religion of the times. And so the Pope is quickly branded as a Taliban. Nevertheless, no one here need fear him. Because he does not come to Berlin as a crusader. He will not set the Reichstag on fire, and has no intention of turning the clock back to the pre-confessional epoch. Before landing in Tegel it is much more apropos to remember how powerless he is.

At his arrival, the bells of all Catholic churches ring through-out the German capital. He cannot make use of the entire Church as he pleases. At his consecration as Bishop of Munich in 1977 he explained: "The bishop does not act in his own name. Rather, he is the trustee of another, Jesus Christ and His Church. He cannot, therefore, change his mind at will, or intervene in support of one thing today and another thing tomorrow—all depending on how convenient it seems. He is not there to dis-seminate his private ideas; rather he is instead an envoy who has to deliver a message that is greater than himself. By this fidelity he is measured; this is his mission." At that time he was fifty years old. But nothing about that mission has changed for him since he became Bishop of Rome and Successor of Peter.

The conversation of German Catholics among themselves and with Rome must therefore be conducted the same way as the discussion of the Protestant churches with the Catholic Church: not only a dialogue that does not forbid certain ideas, but initially one that actually commands them. Reflecting precisely on the fact that the Pope cannot possibly give in to German grievances and complaints in the great majority of cases. That far exceeds his competence. The Catholic Church does not belong to him. He belongs to the Universal Catholic Church with Her Creed and Tradition, which he must serve and not vice versa. An image of the pope that sees him as an all-powerful tyrant, who is consequently to be criticized if he does not willingly satisfy every wish and whim of fickle majorities, leads to utter madness. He simply cannot do what the Tradition and doctrine of the Catholic Church forbid him to do.

What he wants and is trying to do, however, is something greater and so to speak impossible. He described this project shortly after his election in a speech to the Roman Curia on December 22, 2005 — a project to which he has since held fast with remarkable consistency as the intrinsic master plan of his pontificate. He responds to the many ruptures with tradition in recent Church history, which every Catholic can plainly see and can often reach out and touch since the Second Vatican Council, by presenting the radical demand for a "hermeneutic of continuity." This sounds more complicated than it is. Essentially it means: the Catholic Church can neither resign Herself to the ruptures that afflict Her, nor approve of them under any circumstance. Rather,

She must insist on Her unbroken identity and continuity, right back to Her beginning in Jesus Christ's sacrifice on the Cross. The Catholic Church after the Second Vatican Council is therefore the same as before the Council. Those who want to recognize two churches here go astray, whether they are traditionalists who do not want to recognize the Council, or liberals who venerate the break with tradition almost as a new revelation.

It was an extremely lonely and daring adventure that he undertook. But the systematic and radical interpretation of broken Church history as a continuum quickly put on his agenda not only an active process of reconciliation with the conservative Society of Saint Pius X, but also, with the utmost logical consistency, a whole new understanding of the events of the Reformation. This is why, in the Evangelical-Lutheran churches, everyone is well advised to understand in depth the difficult reconciliation of the "supreme bridge builder" from Rome with the traditionalists (the youngest schismatics) as a kind of ecumenical pilot project. A project that is not sufficient in itself but aims at ever greater challenges of reconciliation.

For the Pope from the land of the Reformation, however, this is ecumenism pure and simple. Already in his first message after being elected Pope, he declared that his "principal obligation" was "to work with all his might to restore full and visible unity for all disciples of Christ." Everyone may take this quite seriously. For Benedict XVI, ecumenism is not just any option. It is the only alternative. He did not hope, however, nor did he expect to overcome the rupture as a result or a fruit of documents produced by a committee, but as something that deep down has already reached the goal — as John Paul II wrote to him in 2000 in the logbook of the Church's ship sailing the rough seas of the future: "At the end of the second millennium, the Church once again became a Church of martyrs. The witness for Christ even to the shedding of blood has become the common inheritance of Catholics, Orthodox, Anglicans, and Protestants. The ecumenism of the martyrs and the communion of saints speak louder than the agents of schism." People like Edith Stein and Martin Bonhoeffer are above all examples also for Pope Benedict XVI of "how we make progress in ecumenism." Ecumenism of the love of the Church and of our common origin in God.

Therefore in Berlin, Erfurt, and Freiburg, he will do above all what Jesus already commissioned Peter to do: "Confirm your brethren." The hot potatoes that he will take up are these: holiness of life, worship of God. God first in everything! Among the German Catholics, he will seek to make the concerns of the universal Church heard. For Germans in general, who have been struggling with their identity for centuries, he will at least try, like a good history teacher, to shed new light on where they come from. Naturally, it will be worthwhile listening to him attentively. He will remind those elected representatives who seek to keep their distance about the preamble of the German *Grundgesetz*, in which the German nation, "conscious of its responsibility to God and men," has received its most fortunate constitution in our history. For that lesson a little tutoring and detention couldn't hurt.

The focal point of the journey, however, will be Erfurt, the city in which Luther entered the priestly ministry of the Catholic Church. Never before has a pope come so close to encountering the reformer. There are sure to be even more surprises. For in many respects our days are not unlike the situation of the early sixteenth century. Then, as now, the world experienced a revolution in the means of communication, to such a dramatic extent today, however, that the Pope not long ago spoke of the quasi-"prehistoric" times in which he was ordained a priest in 1951. But this origin in the "prehistoric period," and a kind of new homelessness in the age of increasingly breathless acceleration, now affects a majority of Germany's adult population, whether Catholic, Protestant, or godless.

That is why it would be wise to dim the expectations of this historical journey a bit today, despite all the excitement in the run-up. Playing on his home turf does not immediately translate into a home game for the Pope. The hardships of this journey are unusual. In four days he will give seventeen speeches. Only in Jerusalem was his program more compressed. Why does he take it all on? He wanted it that way. He didn't wish to turn down this invitation or the challenge.

Approaching to Land—Berlin, September 22, 2011

Glorious weather shines over Rome's Ciampino Airport during the farewell ceremony before the Pope departs on his the third journey to his homeland, whose kings for centuries could become emperors only if they were crowned and anointed once again in Rome. In those days, the German kings could be crowned only by the pope, who now returns as pilgrim and teacher, crossing mountains to visit now-democratic Germany. Four thousand journalists have been accredited for the event in Berlin. At 8:00 a.m. the little man in white emerges, entourage in tow, from the airport terminal, bids farewell with a handshake to cardinals in scarlet, bishops in violet, and civil authorities in black; then passes slowly, step by step, along the gangway. He is already feeling his way into this complicated journey.

At 8:20 the plane finally taxis, lifts off in the morning sun, then casts its shadow on the fields far below in a great arc back to the city, over the Baths of Caracalla and the Circus Maximus. The dome of Saint Peter's Basilica glistens portside in the morning sun, already looking quite small before the pilot heads north, toward the Austrian border, then over the Czech Republic toward the German capital. Even before breakfast, most of my journalist colleagues have wolfed down the manuscripts of the four speeches that the Pope will present to the Federal President, the German Parliament, and to representatives of the Jewish community in the Olympic Stadium this evening. Disappointment is spreading. The papers provide "no special reports" for the great carousel of the perpetual news cycle. Nothing about the presumed current topic of a looming Church schism in Germany, even less about the abuse of minors by clergy, nothing at all.

Fresh snow lies below us in the Alps. The summer is over. Clouds cover the country at 9:15 a.m. as Benedict XVI walks to the back of the plane with cautious steps, toward the representatives of the media. Cameras flash like lightning about him, microphones whistle. Is his left eye inflamed? He is standing upright but appears stricken. By the exertion ahead of him? He looks one or another reporter in the eye calmly and answers the first question—in German—recalling the poet Hölderlin, and how much he, as Pope, still feels like a German. His birth has made him a German forever, a part of the country to which he feels so deeply connected, not least to the language in which his mother had introduced him to the secrets of existence. Germany was his destiny, which he gladly accepted. That is one thing. But as a Christian, he was also born again into a new nation, into the eschatological "people taken from all peoples," the "*Civitas Dei*," the global City of God. This is the Church of God, in which he now bears the "supreme responsibility." A quiet beginning to an enormous claim, which he conveys as something perfectly self-evident, as a key note for all that he intends to say and do with his invitation during the next three days: to invite all, in this "dramatic situation," to a "public discussion" about the future of the continent, the geographic and historical center of which is Germany.

He neither falters nor wavers at the next question from the litany of hot-button issues from condoms to contraception: what does he say about cases of clerical abuse and how this scandal drives people out of the Church? He has already answered it on his travels to Malta, Fatima, and Glasgow, and yet he still does not treat it with any sort of routine but with a righteous indignation that grips him every time he merely thinks of it. He can understand each person who as a result of this unbelievable scandal would turn his back on the Church. He replies soberly, without beating around the bush. But we should also ask about the crisis of the Church's image and of alienation in general, which needs to be healed. Where God vanishes from memory, the Church can no longer be recognized as "the most beautiful gift of God," which he will praise that same evening in the Olympic Stadium as coming through all the convulsions solid as a rock — even if in this "net of God" the bad fish are caught along with the good. And what does he say about the protests in Germany against the pope? What is he supposed to have against it? In a free country there is a right to protest. He has experienced and been familiar with protest against his offices for decades, and he also knows the reasons which in Germany have prompted a protest against Rome and the Pope for centuries. To the fourth question, he admits, in conclusion, that he is filled with joy as he looks forward to the meeting in Erfurt with Lutheran-Evangelical sisters and brothers.

Once in German airspace, the Luftwaffe's Eurofighters take over escorting the papal plane, in an airborne ballet in which they follow the sway of the wings like a baton. Meanwhile on board, a debate in various languages begins over whom and what the Successor of Peter the Fisherman could possibly have meant by the "bad fish." While still high above the clouds, the first answers to that question are input into the computers of the news agencies. During the landing at Tegel the flags of Germany and the Vatican flutter in the wind as if they were sails. Immediately the Pope takes hold of his zuchetto — the white cap — to keep the wind from blowing it away. The white mozetta over his cassock billows over his head. Policemen wave from the edge of the tarmac. To them — indeed, to all Germans — the groggy Pontiff with the inflamed eye wishes over the next few days to show "the human Face of God," just as he said with his final words to the media earlier.

Heart to Heart — Berlin, Erfurt, Etzelsbach — September 23, 2011

Sheets of rain pelted Berlin's West End. Then suddenly the sky cleared in a mysterious reversal of light. Silky pink and mauve clouds drifted through the pale sky like so many veils above the open oval of the Olympic Stadium, while below, on the altar platform erected for the occasion, Archbishop Woelki greeted the Pope and 70,000 pilgrims, recalling that Berlin, which is so often called pagan, had given Germany most of her martyrs in the twentieth century. "We shall carry on this witness," said the new chief shepherd of Berlin, and he gave Benedict XVI a "Plötzensee Diptych," a plaque on which are written in gold the names of the martyrs who shed their blood in the horror house of the Nazis, where, between 1934 and 1945, exactly 2,891 people went to their deaths at the gallows or the guillotine — most of them because they had resisted injustice.

Not even an hour before in the Reichstag he had recalled this right to resistance, which sometimes must become a duty to oppose "godless laws," even at the cost of one's life. Now it was the Stadium's turn to shine through the oval roof into the dark sky. Floodlights spilled all over the arena. The Pope's speech in the Bundestag had rent the skies above Germany's media. The editorialists outdid themselves in enthusiastic initial commentaries. The same Pope who only this morning had begun his journey still a little groggy and with an irritated left eye, had finally caught his stride. His voice no longer trembled. The trip has reached its operating speed.

After he had reminded the Jewish community in a separate meeting—still in the Bundestag!—that for Christians, "salvation comes from the Jews," as John the Evangelist said, on Friday morning in the Apostolic Nunciature in Kreuzberg he defended in the presence of the Muslims the rightful claim to an eminently public dimension of religion, "even if this is sometimes interpreted as a provocation." At the same time, he reminded them that the essential impulses of the German Constitution, to which today all Germany's Muslims too owe their dignity in freedom, derived from the inspirational force "of the Christian image of man."

Yet the dialogue among Christians is sometimes more difficult, as was evident in the crowd of journalists who were already waiting for the Pope in Erfurt. The city preserves well-weathered foundations of German history, where the last era of dictatorship once again beaded up like acid rain on the oxidized copper roofs of the *Mariendom*, the cathedral of Our Lady. It is the intrinsic aim of this journey, as the Pope said back in the airplane, to meet the "brothers and sisters" of the Lutheran church in the city where Martin Luther (against his father's will) studied theology, was ordained a priest, and said his first Mass. The Pope had insisted on making a great deal of room in his extremely tight schedule for these encounters in particular.

Is it a fateful day? Erfurt in autumn. The chestnut trees look to be changing their color. Clouds chase high above the red roofs of Luther's Augustinian convent, in which Benedict XVI almost haltingly confesses how Luther's questions prey on his mind, too: "How do I find a living God?" And "What drives Christ?" The Pope identifies with Martin Luther! He invites both Catholics and Protestants to re-examine the question of God in the tsunami of secularization, "in which the absence of God in our society becomes ever more oppressive," and where for that reason we must also pose to ourselves again—like Luther!—the question of sin. Whether our mistakes "are in fact really so small" as we like to suppose of ourselves day by day. It has been a long time since anyone has taken up Martin Luther's "burning questions." For Benedict XVI these are decisive questions for our days too: What does God think of me? How do I stand before God? In the presence of the God who has "shown us His Face."

With these reflections is he not just dodging the urgent questions of ecumenism? He asks the question himself and immediately gives the answer. After all that Christians have preserved in common and rediscovered and achieved and regained by ecumenism, the important thing now is for us to be aware of the danger that everything could be lost again in another so to speak unnoticed cultural revolution. At the beginning of the new millennium, Christians—whether Catholics or Protestants—suddenly run the common risk of losing their irreplaceable foundations. Thus, before the Protestant and political elite of Germany he once again takes up the theme that he had already developed on Thursday at the Bundestag, by sounding the alarm that the departure from natural law as the great European legal tradition will conjure up consequences of totally unsuspected proportions "for the criteria of human existence."

This is not some routine meeting or a ceremonial act of a cleric. The little man in white from Rome speaks softly, but firmly, not telling people what they want to hear, but rather speaking honestly as brothers do together, knowing that they cannot get away from each other. The day has brought renewed earnestness to ecumenical dialogue and a re-adjustment to all false expectations. "The faith of Christians is not based on some calculation of advantages and disadvantages. A self-made faith is worthless. Faith is not something we think up or negotiate. It is the foundation on which we live." All the Pope's talks during these days make the same appeal, repeatedly: to bring about a new awareness of this foundation, in a dramatic time, in necessary ecumenical dialogue together.

Nevertheless, the main concept that runs through his speeches in Germany since his landing at Tegel is not a lament. It is the "heart" that makes a string of pearls out of the guiding thread of his discourse to each audience. It is the "understanding heart" that Solomon had desired when he could have wished for anything from God, and which the Pope now desires and expects of his countrymen in prayer at this "historic hour" at the German Bundestag. With the prophet Ezekiel he prays in the Olympic Stadium for the "living heart of flesh and blood" to take away and to replace "the heart of stone from our breast." These are questions which Luther once "took to heart," and the Pope wishes that Christians of the modern era would once again take them to heart so as to answer them anew together. Yet he describes in the most striking way the situation of separated Christians after the ecumenical meeting in Erfurt, not with a new line from Luther, but in a meditation on the Pietà in Etzelsbach, an ancient Marian shrine to which the helicopters of the Luftwaffe bring him that evening, where he prays Evening Prayer from the liturgy of the hours of the old Church. "In most representations of the Pietà, the expired Jesus lies with his head to the left. The viewer can thus see the wound in the side of the Crucified," he explains to the pilgrims. "In this case, however, that wound is hidden, because the dead body is oriented instead to the other side. It seems to me that this representation conceals a profound meaning, which only becomes evident in quiet contemplation. In this grace-filled image the hearts of Jesus and his Mother are turned to each other. They are close to each other." The pierced heart of the Son pressed to the throbbing heart of the Mother. During these days it beats louder and louder.

Year of Faith—Rome, October 23, 2011

It is a truism. Authors who want to be read know that they absolutely have to write. They cannot hope for overwhelming numbers of readers who understand allusions to connections that the author has studied, possibly for years. Maybe this sort of education served up incidentally was never more than an elitist obsession. But not in one field. For in Europe there was a frame of reference for centuries, about which you could toss all sorts of balls to someone at any stage of education, from childhood to old age, and he would catch them as a matter of course. There was a shared narrative in the West, which everyone understood without translation and passed along even when he rebelled against it. This was, essentially, the ancient account of the life and death of Jesus of Nazareth and of His resurrection from the dead on the third day. This was the Christian profession of faith, as it was laid down in the year 325 in Nicea (modern Iznik in Turkey) at the first Ecumenical Council of 318 bishops and some 2,000 other participants — including the Emperor Constantine: "We believe in one God, the Father, the almighty, creator of heaven and earth, and of all things visible and invisible. And in one Lord, Jesus Christ, the only begotten Son of God, born of the Father before all ages: God from God, Light from Light, true God from true God." And so on. But wait!

For who knows what follows? How many educated readers no longer know this short constitutional preamble of Christianity by heart? How many simply have not learned the Creed, as though it were Latin or ancient Greek, or another old, dead language? How many were never taught it by their parents or teachers? At a time when Christian theologians have risen to higher heights and descended to lower depths than the human mind has ever explored, the water table of Christians' knowledge of their fundamentals has dropped dramatically. Others talk about the faith all but evaporating in broad sectors of formerly Christian nations. It amounts to the same thing.

This selfsame faith, though, had long been acknowledged as a frame of reference, even for the mortal enemies of the Christians — like the Soviets or Nazis — whom they wanted "to exterminate, root and branch," and for that purpose had concocted fantastic mimicries as counter-religions. Nevertheless, Christian faith remained, in many respects, the social cement. Thus, even after the Second World War, there emerged from this original foundation vital impulses for the development of a reconciled Europe. Afterward, though, within two generations, the old cement has crumbled into dust. Nowadays things often get rubber-stamped that even the Nazis could not have achieved so easily — like the removal of the cross from public places. Not infrequently, as Pope

Benedict wrote last week, it happens that Christians "continue to regard the faith as a self-evident presupposition of life in general. In reality, however, not only is this presupposition no longer accepted in this form, but it is often even denied. While it was possible in the past to recognize a uniform cultural fabric that widely accepted as its point of reference the contents of the faith and the values inspired by them, that no longer appears to be the case in many parts of society due to a profound crisis of faith that has befallen so many." In Germany, he even spoke of an "eclipse of God" on account of which he proclaimed a "Year of Faith" from 2012 to 2013, "in order to lead the entire Church through a period of rediscovery of the faith." It is an emergency program "at a moment when mankind is experiencing profound changes."

The last "Year of Faith" was declared by Paul VI in 1968. The situation for Christianity today, however, seems even more dramatic than the great upheavals of that year. In an epoch of enormous uncertainty, the Pope is trying to buck the trend of regional cooking shows and make a pitch for the taste and recipe of a food that "does not spoil and endures to eternal life." It is a missionary project no longer to foreign lands but into the interior of Christendom, back to the "radical newness of the resurrection" of Christ, which "expands hearts with hope." It is a course correction for the Church, which he teaches by this initiative that faith is never a possession, but can live and thrive only in the act of faith.

As Benedict of Nursia once salvaged for Europe in his monasteries the culture of antiquity from the chaos of the barbarian invasions, so too Benedict XVI now intends, during the stormy revolution at the onset of the Information Age, to transmit to future generations the "knowledge of the faith," the "formation of Christians" and the faith as a creative and "courageous act of freedom," "not as a theory, but as an encounter with a person": with God made man.

"*Allahu akbar!*" is the slogan of the Arab Spring. In the autumn of the West, on the other hand, the Pope now wants to give a new account of the whole faith of Christians and to spread it to Generation Facebook in Europe, America, Africa, Asia and Australia. An impossible undertaking? To be sure. Only it does not seem hopeless, as we know from Benedict of Nursia. In the seventh year of his pontificate, Benedict XVI now intends, in any event, to open an ecumenical elementary school of faith, where the first thing on the old teacher's lesson plan is a lesson on the identity of the faithful, who "become stronger by believing."

Vatileaks, the Pope's Valet, and a Laboratory of Peace in Beirut — 2012

Friend of the little friends — Rome, April 19, 2012
Benedict XVI walks with a cane. No wonder, given the eighty-five years that he completes today [April 16]. The wonder is, rather, that seven years after his election as Pope he has not long since been on his last legs. The burden of his office is enormous, in addition to the usual wear and tear on the body in old age. For years now his brother Georg has been demonstrating all that might yet happen to him. The hip joint, the eyes, the ears, all the bones. It hurts, sometimes here and sometimes there. Benedict XVI is healthy and leads an extremely reasonable, well-ordered life, yet now the man, who has always been rather delicate, has become one of the oldest popes ever. His predecessor, John Paul II, the Pope with the athlete's heart, died six weeks before he turned eighty-five. Benedict XVI overtook "God's marathon man" in March.

He is really old now, despite all the hours in which he seems ever younger, for instance in the afternoon of March 24, when he met with the children on the Plaza de la Paz in Guanajuato, Mexico. The square was bursting at the seams. Orchestra, children's choirs, trumpets, nothing that makes a din was missing. The Pope had already got over and done with a routine speech in Spanish to the President of the Republic and the cardinals and bishops of Mexico at the airport after the long-distance flight from Rome, when he turned to the children: "Dear Young People, I am happy ... to see your smiling faces as you fill this beautiful square. You have a very special place in the Pope's heart.... Today we are full of jubilation, and this is important. God wants us to be happy always.... If we allow the love of Christ to change our heart, then we can change the world. This is the secret of authentic happiness." All the exhaustion seemed to be wiped away. He not only looked quite alert, he was. According to his inner clock, however, it was exactly 2:30 in the morning, Roman time. "You, my dear young friends, are not alone." He was happy, that was clear, and that of course is not always the case.

For this "friend of the young friends" has remained a "Doctor of the Church" and a missionary and always a pastor of souls. He was a professor. Now he is Bishop of Rome and monarch of the Vatican State. Above all, however, as successor of the Apostle Peter for seven years he has been the supreme shepherd of an immensely large flock of Catholics, which often threatens to scatter in all directions. But there is no career training for the papacy. It cannot be learned. And Joseph Ratzinger never learned to pull strings, to recruit a power base or to seek advantage by networking, neither as Archbishop of Munich nor as head of the Congregation for the Doctrine of the Faith in Rome. That is foreign to his nature. In this sense he has remained to this day an outsider. Already at the age of thirty-one he demanded a radical conversion of the Church "from power, from cronyism, from false appearances, from mammon, from deceit and self-deception," decades before German Catholics began to wonder, after his concert hall speech in Freiburg last autumn, what he might have meant by "becoming unworldly," which as he said farewell he recommended to the Church in Germany as a remedy for its necessary renewal — a cause that has been dear to his heart since the Council. Is that otherworldly? Is he otherworldly? Only in a certain respect. In fact he did not play along with many games. He always saw everything.

He never had a career plan, either, although many consider that humanly impossible. That is why even today he often seems like an amateur. For years now he has usually called to his side people whom he knows and trusts, but no cunning tacticians, politicians, or administrative geniuses. Spectacular breakdowns, with which his pontificate has by now been blessed, along with his three Encyclicals, his travels and books about Jesus of Nazareth, are thus almost pre-programmed, certainly from the perspective of a media-driven world in which the Christian Creed of Nicea from the year 325 no longer has any meaning whatsoever — except that it is still bothersome. Thus the older this friend of the young friends becomes, in the twilight of post-modernity, the more he himself seems like a Little Prince from another planet, like a *Wunderkind* who always pursues his goals directly, without looking to the left or to the right, with remarkable endurance, regardless of any success or failure.

Since the 1980s he has pursued unwaveringly the reconciliation process with the conservative Society of Saint Pius X — in which, contrary to all historical and human probability, he has consistently tried to prevent a final schism of the Catholic Church. No one has waged as purposefully as he the battle against abuse of any sort and for the unreserved illumination of this dark side of the Church. He cannot be bribed: even his keenest critics and enemies must acknowledge this (and there has been no lack of them throughout his lifetime); nevertheless, this did not make him a zealous Jacobin. What his friends and opponents inside and outside the Church can expect of him in the future too, however, was as plainly evident in recent days in the great liturgy of Good Friday and Easter Sunday as in an open book.

These celebrations form the high point of the Church year, starting with Palm Sunday on Saint Peter's Square and continuing until the papal blessing in more than sixty languages upon the city of Rome and the whole world (*urbi et orbi*) on Easter Sunday—and they are exceedingly arduous. Nowhere can the Pope be replaced by a delegate, neither in the Lateran nor at night at the Colosseum nor in Saint Peter's Basilica. The ceremonies demand great discipline, for instance "the Memorial of the Passion and Death of the Lord" on Good Friday, in which the complete Passion according to John is not only read aloud, but sung word for word in Latin. This devotion requires standing—not sitting—for forty minutes. Only the notice of Christ's death allows those in attendance to kneel down briefly. As he made the exertion this year, the Pope amazed even the Swiss Guards with how calmly he persisted in front of them with his hands folded, like one of them, as though keeping watch, in royal purple, without the slightest distraction, like an Indian fakir in meditation. Even the masters of ceremonies at his right and his left seemed nervous this time in comparison to the old man. Between them the Pope stood like a tree. The Catholic Church can expect this composed calm from him in the future as well.

The following night, however, it was as though he would nevertheless announce his legacy now, when in his homily he explained how God's recognizability in the light of the Easter Vigil is the unique selling point of Christianity. This was and is his lifelong theme. The "unconquered light of God's illumination" is what experienced a second, new creation in the Easter Vigil; as early as 1959 he published a sensational essay about this in the journal *Hochland*. Now for his Easter greeting he selected a painting of the Easter event by Johann Heinrich Tischbein from the year 1763, in which a brightly shining Christ steps out of the tomb into the dawn of the first Easter day—in a sort of reversal of Plato's allegory of the cave. It is a painted vision. "Let us pray to the Lord at this time," he now exclaimed, "that through the Church, Christ's radiant Face may enter our world."

He is not the head of a business firm. His latitude for decision-making is very limited, light years away from the infallible omnipotence that is usually ascribed to him. We should imagine the Pope instead as the president of a foundation, in which he knows that he is unconditionally obliged, not by a private faith, but by the founder's institutional will.

The board of directors of this foundation cannot and will never make this deposit of faith subject to negotiation: the common faith of untold millions over many centuries in a unique amalgam of identity and continuity. "I have never tried," he explained to his interviewer Peter Seewald back in 1996, "to create a system of my own, an individual theology. What is specific, if you want to call it that, is that I simply want to think in communion with the faith of the Church, and that means above all to think in communion with the great thinkers of the faith." Nothing about that has changed. This framework for the former theologian of the heady days of the Council will remain his guideline as Pope and in the future for judging whether a demand for reform is justified or not.

When he looks down from his window onto Saint Peter's Square, he always glances at the obelisk that Peter once saw when he was crucified upside-down there below in Nero's Circus. The Vatican Hill, which is so splendidly built up, is nothing other than the Gallows Hill of the first pope. This view made Benedict XVI fearless long ago. As the successor of Peter he will not and does not want to escape his obligations alive. This makes him freer than many suspect, precisely in his native land. Yes, he walks with a cane now. But it is above all a shepherd's staff, with which the eighty-five-year-old man holds together over a billion Catholics worldwide.

Paoletto, the Pope's valet — Rome, May 25, 2012

It probably grieved the Pope very, very much and will continue to cause him pain. And not only him. Paolo Gabriele was until now — they say — known in the Vatican as a pious man. Above all, however, he was part of the so-called papal family, the closest circle around the *Santo Padre*, in which he was even jokingly called "Paulie" (Paoletto). He was the friendly, very well-mannered valet and majordomo of His Holiness, who often sat in the front seat in the Pope's open Mercedes (with the license plate SCV 1 [Vatican City State 1]) beside the driver and in front of the private secretary Georg Gänswein. He was one of the few laymen who had access to the papal *appartamento*. The Vatican citizen helped the Pope as he got up in the morning and dressed. He was his attendant during audiences. He served the midday meal and sat at the table with the others. In the evening he prepared the Pope's room for a night of rest. He accompanied him on his journeys and had access to all the keys of the Pontiff's most private world. But now, according to reliable Vatican sources, he was arrested by the Vatican gendarmes on Thursday afternoon for the continued betrayal of secrets and as of Friday morning is being interrogated by the Vatican public prosecutor. Basically he has pleaded guilty. Given the evidence, we can rule out the possibility that this is merely about a hastily selected and arrested scapegoat for the disappearance of documents from the Pope's desk which has been going on for months—a theory being aired in parts of the Italian press.

When he was arrested he was in the unauthorized possession of confidential files, which would also have made it difficult for him to deny the charges. For it was not just one paper in his briefcase, but rather a whole series of classified documents that were found in his apartment and, to make matters worse for him, fit neatly into a series of around thirty confidential documents from the Pope's desk that since last week have adorned in facsimile a book-length exposé by the journalist Gianluigi Nuzzi with the eloquent title: *Sua Santità: Le carte segrete di Benedetto XVI* (His Holiness: The secret papers of Benedict XVI). This is a case of "theft," a communiqué from the Vatican said, for which those responsible will be called to account. This process has now obviously begun. The next few weeks will show whether after "Paulie's" arrest more secret papers of the Pope are made public in the future. In any case, since the beginning of the year various deliberate indiscretions from the Vatican had grown to such proportions that months ago the spokesman from the Press Office, Father Federico Lombardi, S.J., had already coined the term "Vatileaks" for the place that was not watertight.

This is an upsetting disclosure, most of all for Benedict XVI, of course. It will be little help or consolation to him as a theologian that he has been familiar since his First Holy Communion with the idea that ever since Judas the worst betrayer usually sits with you at table. On the other hand, though, the painful process of clearing up the matter, despite the serious, personal breach of confidence, may also give him some satisfaction. The arrest promises not only to put an end to the terrible mistrust sown in the halls of the papal palace. It is also a relatively swift reward for a step that he took casually several weeks ago: entrusting the criminal case to an investigatory commission made up of three retired cardinals. They are the Most Reverend Lords Julian Herranz (82), Jozef Tomko (88) and Salvatore De Giorgi (82), and this spectacularly successful manhunt should probably be attributed now to their deductive skills and common sense. Now, at any rate, we await their answer to the trickiest question, the original criminologist's brain teaser: *Cui bono?* "Who profited by all this?"

Man's heart is an abyss—Rome, July 15, 2012

Rumors in Rome. Everyone is puzzling it over. One man sits in jail. The Pope's former valet, Paolo Gabriele, will remain a few days more under arrest, the Vatican spokesman Father Federico Lombardi announced on Thursday—after the completion of the fifty-day interval that the Vatican State foresees for pre-trial detention. The valet, Lombardi says, is still the only suspect. Accomplices are unknown. Father Lombardi is a reliable man of honor. As far as the actionable part of the case is concerned, in which Gabriele over a long period of time copied innumerable confidential documents from the Pope's residence and handed them on to various others, there is little more to be said. From the perspective of those who are conducting the judicial investigation, the document thief, who was caught with both hands "*nella marmellata*" ("in the marmalade") is still the only guilty party.

Behind—or rather before—the House of Justice, human nature however built the House of Intrigue, Envy, and Wickedness. Here we are speaking not about criminal acts but about all-too-human abysses. The book *Sua Santità* by the muckraker Gianluigi Nuzzi provides a sort of master key to this house with many rooms.

After a series of confidential documents that were leaked from the Vatican to the Italian press since the beginning of this year, Nuzzi since May 17 has exploited commercially an enormous quantity of letters from the Pope's desk. "The rules of transparency should apply to the Church too," he justifies his procedure, because "secrecy is the antechamber of doubt and mistrust." But now the transparency that he invokes is turning against his own sources.

In his book he gave them the collective name "Maria." Who or what is this—a person or a code name? He says that they are "practicing Catholics who work or live in the Vatican and are trusted enough that they have access to confidential documents." Nuzzi will always be grateful to these "little heroes of the book." With his thanks, however, they will not be able to buy much for themselves now. First of all Paolo "Paoletto" Gabriele, his main supplier, whom he mentioned in passing on page 11 and put behind bars with the careless publication of an account statement—on page 311—because there is no doubt that he alone could have pilfered this paper.

The Secretary of State, Cardinal Bertone, recently declared that Benedict XVI "loved Paoletto like a son." Nevertheless, Paulie started years ago to steal from him like a raven. Not jewels, though; just papers. Very secret papers that he carried out of the papal chambers—including German letters that he himself could not even read. That is one of the first findings of an investigative commission made up of three elderly cardinals, whom the Pope appointed to clear up the betrayal, so as to be able to interrogate not only Nuzzi's "little heroes" but anyone in the Vatican, if necessary. Cardinals are not obliged to speak to and answer anyone but cardinals.

Among them the investigations continue according to a routine, Father Lombardi repeats in his dry briefings, during which he turns up his nose as though he were trying to balance his glasses in front of his eyes again when they slip down. There are four or five interrogations per week in these hot summer days in Rome, of clerics as well as laymen, whereby the "interrogation of a person is not yet synonymous with any suspicion," as Lombardi emphasizes.

In parallel to this, the state prosecutor continues its investigation. The case involves not only grand theft, but also high treason, which according to Article III, paragraph 2, of the Vatican Constitution can incur in the case of the deliberate breach of a "papal secret" even the punishment of excommunication. Gabriele himself is said to be cooperating; he is calm and "prays a lot," as Father Lombardi said on Thursday. Yet even if the "raven" should "sing" only hesitantly, the documents found on him, his confiscated personal computer and his smartphone speak volumes, of course, about his contacts and his background.

And Nuzzi's book keeps singing like a nightingale; criminologist-theologians are studying it as critically as trained exegetes read the Bible. Accordingly, many circumstances in the case surrounding the person of the document thief are even now falling together like a puzzle. For "Paoletto" Gabriele lacks all that it takes to be a central figure. Everyone who knows him—and many people in and around the Vatican do—describe him as a modest, simple, pious man. He did his work well. Always proper.

A *"bella figura"* [someone who is careful to make a nice impression]. It hardly mattered that his expression was a bit grim, although today many people notice it when they look at photos of him. He wanted to be a *"buonista,"* a good guy.

In the Vatican his career began as a custodial worker; he cleaned the marble floors of Saint Peter's Basilica and of the *Sacri Palazzi*, until a certain Monsignor Paolo Sardi recommended him to Archbishop James Harvey, the Prefect of the Papal Household. For Gabriele it was like winning the lottery. In 2006 he became the successor of the legendary majordomo Angelo Gugel, although after a trial period the latter considered him inexperienced and was unwilling to recommend him for this service. The valet's work is an extremely varied half-day job for a highly trusted employee, for which Gabriele was remunerated, in addition to his pay, with a nice servant's apartment in a house behind the Church of Saint Anne within the walls of the Vatican — directly adjacent to the red wall with the high fence — for himself, his wife and their three children. This service demands a mature character, which Gabriele obviously did not have.

And so he is now in custody two blocks away in the barracks of the gendarmerie under strict supervision. Yet even now he still wants to go to Mass on Sundays — accompanied by gendarmes but without handcuffs — and to do that he will probably also want to go to confession, like all genuine sinners, of which the Catholic Church does in fact consist. All who know him are convinced that he must have acted out of a pious conviction and that he was probably confirmed in it.

He was unmasked on Tuesday evening, May 22, and it is noteworthy that he did not remove even one of the many incriminating documents in his residence until his arrest on Wednesday evening (May 23). A search of the house may have seemed to him altogether unlikely. He cannot have relied on the slowly grinding mills of the extremely unhurried Vatican. The more likely hypothesis is that he must have relied on very high protection within the Vatican.

Equally revealing was the fact that a few days after Gabriele was unmasked by the papal private secretary, Georg Gänswein, the "Vatileaks" campaign against the Vatican leadership, which had been going on for months, suddenly very publicly and purposefully turned into blackmail of that same secretary, who was threatened by an anonymous author in *La Repubblica* with further disclosures, unless the Pope quickly got rid of his "inept coworkers" (*collaboratori inetti*).

It was as though one of Nuzzi's brave "little heroes" suddenly lost his nerve. After that, all was quiet on the blackmail front. In his makeshift Vatican "high security prison cell" Gabriele of course heard nothing whatsoever about all this. Whether it has dawned on him behind bars that he was hoodwinked, the court will have to find out during the trial against him that is supposed to begin this autumn. But really, he must have noticed at latest by two weeks before his arrest that something was wrong with the innuendos that misled him to breach confidentiality.

That was when Nuzzi's book with his stolen goods suddenly hit the market to great media fanfare. Had he consoled himself with the thought that the Vatican investigators might just be hunting for a fictitious female spy named "Maria"? No wonder speculations about factions within the Curia flourished. The great big intrigue in the upper echelons: that, of course, is the sort of thing that many find lip-smacking good. But what if it were different this time—smaller, pettier?

Let's just stick with what is plain for all to see; let us follow a bit the trails that the investigators too are following. Where did Gabriele live, with whom did he speak, with whom was he often meeting? In the afternoons he had a lot of time, and the Italian press says that during that time he ostentatiously maintained "many contacts," with journalists as well as with other citizens of the Vatican State and of Italy. His mobile phone, his voicemail and his e-mail exchanges will reveal a lot about that. The criminologists of the Vatican know their trade just as well as their worldly colleagues.

It takes no sophistication to find out that also living in his house along the Vatican wall is Ingrid Stampa, who appears in Nuzzi's book on pages 6, 14, and 74 as "faithful housekeeper," "unofficial advisor," and "one of the few women to whom the Pontiff listens." (Moreover, on page 74 it is revealed how she became involved in extremely delicate procedures of the Vatican and decisions of the Pope.)

Before and after the termination of Gabriele's service, this neighbor lady was a welcome guest of his wife and children. No one in the Vatican was as close to the master thief as she. "It was an intensive contact," another woman living in the house says knowingly. Everyone behind Saint Anne's Gate knows it — from the officers of the Swiss Guard and the gendarmerie to the postmen, the Augustinians of Saint Anne's parish and the many collaborators at the nearby editorial offices of *L'Osservatore Romano*.

The former personal physician of John Paul II had recommended this musical lady to Cardinal Ratzinger in 1991 as a housekeeper, after his sister Maria died. Since then she has been close to him. Five years ago, however, one could already read also about voices in the halls of the Vatican that called her "*la Papessa*" [the female Pope], because the shy music professor occupied "a scarcely defined independent position in the murky parallelogram of forces in the Secretariat of State" because "in the labyrinth of secret doors she was able to obtain unimpeded access to the Pontiff: as a self-appointed advisor, who apart from any competency has the ear and the soft heart of the Holy Father." That was then.

Today among Vatican watchers there is, in addition, widespread knowledge about Ingrid Stampa's jealousy of any woman or man whom the Pope actually or potentially trusts more than her. In this affliction she is surpassed in Rome probably only by the jealousy of Ratzinger's former secretary and today Curia Bishop Josef Clemens on the other side of Saint Peter's Square, who for years has been unsuccessful at concealing and curbing his downright irrational envy of his successor at the Pope's side. For nineteen years he had served Joseph Ratzinger. The Roman sparrows have been piping from the rooftops for a long time the fact that he regards his successor as an "incompetent collaborator" of the Pontiff. For years now the bishop from Germany, in his jealousy, has found in the ambitious Ingrid Stampa a reliable ally. Therefore she alone took part also in those legendary dinners in his residence on the top floor of the Palazzo del Sant'Uffizio to which the Curia bishop until recently still had the privilege of inviting the Pope three times a year—until this tradition (according to the report of another bishop) was abruptly ended a few weeks ago by Benedict XVI himself with a short note.

Theologically, in contrast, the old papal confidante and former housekeeper has long since been of one heart and one soul with Cardinal Paolo Sardi, with the selfsame Monsignor, therefore, who years ago opened for "Paoletto" Gabriele the door and advancement to the papal palace. This learned prince of the Church from Northern Italy was for many years responsible for the papal addresses, a position with a high occupational risk of imagining occasionally that one is cleverer and more papal than the Pope. One cannot say that he ever was a fan of Joseph Ratzinger's theology, and he is able to get as little from the course that the Pope has set as he can from the latter's tiny handwriting, to put it mildly. Many in the Vatican know all this. The little State is, after all, a big village too. On January 22, 2011, the Pope accepted without further ado the resignation submitted by Cardinal Sardi from his post as vice-chamberlain for reasons of age.

It is not too much to maintain that these three persons—at varying distances—stood with, by, or behind Paolo Gabriele. Of course for this reason alone they will not have been surprised to be included as though automatically in the investigation—and of course the presumption of innocence applies to them all. Consequently they may figure as prominent representatives of the climate in which Paoletto's fingers somehow kept getting longer.

The full background of the systematic theft of documents is therefore—this can be said already—not in the least one-dimensional. Insufficiently complex conspiracy theories do not do justice to the case. The picture that emerges is an amalgam of abuse of trust and a game of hide-and-seek played by various forces which—starting with Gianluigi Nuzzi—for various motives made use of the valet's art of the steal.

He may be a deceived deceiver. Nevertheless, the drama in which he is involved is by no means a comedy. A conspiracy within the Curia? Maybe that too, but only a smidgeon. In any case it is not a coup. No palace revolution. No Dan Brown. It is all much more realistic—and more human: a round-dance of beating hearts full of envy and grudges. More Dostoyevsky than Shakespeare. "*Cor hominis abyssus*" (the heart of man is an abyss), Benedict XVI knows from his favorite theologian, Augustine.

Now he stands shocked in front of a pile of rubble of broken trust, in a devilish trial for a man his age that is not yet over.

Even the old classic question of criminologists, "*cui bono?*" leads in this case into a vacuum: "Who benefits?"

For no one who has been blinded by jealousy asks that question. They all wanted to "help" the Pope, they say—from Gianluigi Nuzzi to Paoletto Gabriele. It is not just a little crazy. It is deranged. A cruel attack of a very special sort on the Pope, who prays for every one of his enemies. Even my mother used to say: "Jealousy [*Eifersucht*] is a passion [*Leidenschaft*] that seeks with zeal [*mit Eifer sucht*] the things that cause suffering [*was Leiden schafft*]," although I don't know where she found that out. This poisonous passion has now touched many in the Vatican, from the "raven" in his cell to Benedict XVI high up in his golden cage, where with the soaring of his mind he often flies as high as a young eagle.

Kafka in Rome—Rome, July 28, 2012

The only man ever known to have been crucified on Saint Peter's Square was—around two thousand years ago—the Apostle Peter. John Paul II came within a hair's breadth of being shot to death here on May 13, 1981. It is no place for executions. Heads do not roll here. Augustin Theiner, the German priest who around the year 1870 purloined and published many documents from the papal secret archives, was merely relieved of his duties. Rudolf von Gerlach, the private chamberlain who during World War I abused the trust of Benedict XV and betrayed him (in order to draw the neutral Vatican into the war on the side of the Axis Powers), was sentenced to imprisonment for life—in absentia, though, because this "raven" had already flown away to Switzerland.

And so today "Paulie" Gabriele, the thieving valet of Benedict XVI, need not trouble his head with any real concerns.

Nevertheless, he and his attorneys should take care not to insult the Pope's intelligence. Last Monday his attorney Carlo Fusco informed startled journalists in the press room of the Holy See that not only had his client stolen from the Pope all by himself, he had been driven to do it by nothing but the "longing" to come to the Pontiff's aid with such "acts of love." The former janitor of Saint Peter's Basilica wanted "to clean up the Church"! There were no players behind the scene. No accomplices. And so, technically speaking, we are supposed to imagine that the case unfolded as follows: One day "Paulie" was walking along the Via della Conciliazione with a briefcase of stolen documents and lost it. Without noticing it. Then by chance the journalist Gianluigi Nuzzi came down the street after him, saw the brief-case, looked inside and said to himself: "Oh! Now I will make a best-seller out of this." No sooner said than done. That is how it must have been.

Therefore it is not so much a plausibility competition that is raging in these hot summer days in Rome over what actually happened behind the betrayal of secrets in the Vatican; instead it is as though Kafka had taken command here since the Pope retreated to Castel Gandolfo in early July. Until the feast of the Assumption of Mary into heaven he is leaving official business in other hands. That does not mean that he is resting. He intends to complete Part Three of his Jesus trilogy, on the childhood and youth of the Son of God from Nazareth — about which the Gospels divulge very little. It is a concern near and dear to his heart.

After all, he intends to portray the Holy Family in this book — and surely for this purpose he will refer also to his own background. "*Ciao, Papa,*" a seven-year-old girl greeted him re-cently in Milan during a question-and-answer session. "I am Cat Tien from Vietnam and would like to know what it was like when you were my age." The old man did not hesitate a second. "To tell the truth, I imagine that in paradise it will be like it was in my childhood." His brother was not the sort that would break his toys. His father was the pillar of justice in the village, whom the atrocities of the two world wars never stained or wounded. His mother and older sister did not idolize the youngest child but lovingly revered him.

In his family he did not become acquainted with evil, but certainly with the sacred, which left a lasting impression on him (and his siblings). At that time, though, he came to know and love the "Holy Family" also, which today is hardly ever mentioned except in mockery. It is quite possible that this came at the expense of a lack of knowledge about human nature, which then always accompanied him even afterward. And an almost proverbial guilelessness. Developmental psychologists will probably be able to confirm something of the sort. That an unhappy youth often leads to later mistrust of everyone—and a happy childhood to a preliminary confidence in every man and woman, as Joseph Ratzinger has shown toward many to a high degree.

Family is sacred to him to this day. This makes him appreciate better the lessons that are being taught him finally at an advanced age. The years of betrayal of trust originating within his papal "family" must have affected him more sorely than the news about the bullets from Ali Ağca's revolver that struck down his predecessor on Saint Peter's Square. He will probably try to cope with this too in his new book. In his homily on June 29 in Saint Peter's Basilica it was as though he revealed a sample of this, from the Book of Wisdom: "Through the devil's envy death entered the world." Later on he explained the obscure passage as follows: "The first dead man in history mentioned by revelation is Abel, who was murdered by his brother Cain. It is related that

God was pleased with Abel's sacrifice and Cain became jealous, because God was happy with his brother." Fraternal jealousy is presented here as the original motive in the human history of calamity [*Unheils-geschichte*]. As a vice from which no well-being [*Heil*] grows.

In any case, it was possible for the document thief to crack the papal firewall only because he belonged to the inner circle, to the "*famiglia.*" Surely he pilfered alone. But not even the most skillful lawyers will manage to pass him off as the mastermind and sole culprit. As we said, he will not have to fear for his head. What is to be feared, however, is damage to the Vatican's credibility through such attempts. For this reason too Benedict XVI will study the report of his cardinalatial commission as carefully as the Bible. Afterward he will react [*reagieren*] and then rule [*regieren*] again. For the moment, though, it is as if Paolo Gabriele somehow was taken in by an absurd mirror image of the Pope's motives. For Benedict XVI does in fact want to clean up the Church. It is one of his chief concerns. He will not make an exception of his own house. He will not cover anything up. No one should fear, therefore, that he will sweep the results of the investigation of this case under the rug — and no one inside or outside of the Vatican should hope for that either.

In the eye of the hurricane — Beirut, September 12, 2012

A bus trip from Jerusalem to Beirut in the last century took maybe six hours. Meanwhile the route has been impossible for decades. Even the Navigator app of the iPhone balks at the task of calculating the virtual itinerary. It is as though the two cities were on different planets. And there is something to that view. Nevertheless, they are both located in the Holy Land, through which the "patriarchs and prophets traveled," as Benedict XVI said on Friday during his most recent journey as a pilgrim. Here "the Savior's cross loomed" above. Syria and Egypt too are reckoned as parts of this Holy Land. The cedars of Lebanon are just as proverbial in the psalms as the beauty of its female inhabitants. King Solomon was in close contact with King Hiram in the present-day city of Tyre, which was already a harbor city at the time of the Phoenicians. Today's Holy Land in its totality, however, is completely torn and consumed by wars and violence, even though the coast in front of Beirut appears, beneath the Pope's Alitalia flight as it comes in for a landing, just as peaceful as it did years ago near Tel Aviv just before he set foot on Israel's soil in Lod Airport.

Now the flight took only three and a half hours from Rome to Beirut, which from nearby Jerusalem is almost unreachable. It can be reached, though, from Damascus, which is even nearer and the point of origin of many thousands of refugees who have streamed into Lebanon in recent weeks and months—from Aleppo and Homs as well, "both Christians and Muslims," as the Pope emphasized while still on the airplane. The war makes no distinction in the universal sorrow that it brings upon mankind.

"No," he said while still in the air, where the plane repeatedly met with heavy turbulence, he was "not afraid." It was as if even the airspace in an alarming way reflected the ghostly Fata Morgana of the atmosphere of war everywhere in the Near East. And the tsunami of violence that afflicts one capital after another down there in the Levant. He never hesitated either, to embark on this journey, he continued. He appeared before the journalists hesitantly but spoke firmly to them when he challenged and invited them to support him in the work for peace for which he set out on this journey. Any kind of fundamentalism is a falsification of religion and perverts its nature into the opposite. The arms trade is also a "serious sin" that feeds numerous conflicts like a pipeline of evil. And the Arab Spring? At this question he did not hesitate for an instant. This awakening can and must be evaluated only in a positive way; it is a cry of the young people for freedom and participation in the life of society.

What the Christians of Lebanon probably expect most from him, though, is an exhortation and encouragement from the head of Christendom to start a Christian Spring in the region, especially at this hour of its particular need. That is why the Pope came, too, and he is doing all he can so as not to disappoint them. In Beirut he lands as though in the eye of the hurricane, fearless as Leo the Great confronting the Huns in Mantua, while U.S. warships cruise along the coast of Libya and a whipped-up mob in Sudan storms the German embassy. Never before during his pontificate have there been more explosive political storms, yet now at Rafiq-Hariri Airport he appears before General Michel Sleiman, President of the Lebanese Republic, and a gathering of the country's elite, and does not mention the word "war" even once in his address during the welcome ceremony.

Instead he invokes right at the beginning this ancient, exemplary country's close connection with the West: as an expression of their bonds and ongoing exchange with Rome and the popes, the patriarchs of the Maronites have always included "Peter" as part of their name. In the coming days, however, he intends to present the cedar state especially to the Near East and to the whole world once again as a "model" of how "within a nation there can exist cooperation between the various churches, ... and at the same time coexistence and respectful dialogue between Christians and their brethren of other religions." Of course, he concedes, this equilibrium, which so many admire as an example, is extremely delicate. And often too it runs the risk of becoming "overstretched" like a valuable old bow. Preserving the ever-endangered Lebanese model of sublime balance among religions, confessions, and ethnic groups is a challenge in which "real moderation and great wisdom are tested." Here he bends the narrative arc to King Solomon, King Hiram's friend, who fervently prayed to God for this very wisdom "of an understanding heart" and received it. It is an arc that leads from Beirut back to Berlin, to his epoch-making speech last September before the German *Bundestag* beneath the cupola of the *Reichstag*. The close coupling of faith to reason (and vice versa) for the architecture of a better and more peaceful future world has become a signature theme of his pontificate. What this means for the Near East he set down in a document with the title *Ecclesia in Medio Oriente*, which he will sign on Friday evening, so as then to present it on Saturday to the world as a "roadmap" for the coming years.

Before him, President Sleiman (in English: Solomon) also recalled the indispensable "Christian and Muslim coexistence to preserve the historical calling of Lebanon's role," which affects "all the peoples of the Levant." An invention made here in pre-historic times was "the alphabet for structuring thoughts," which the land of the Phoenicians presented to the West and to the whole world as a means of communication and mutual understanding. Drum rolls frame the speeches. The sea sparkles faintly behind Rafiq Hariri Airport. Wind musses the Pontiff's hair. As a wise precaution, the magazines of ammunition were removed from the automatic weapons of the soldiers who parade past the Pope at the conclusion.

Laboratory of peace — Beirut, September 15, 2012

"Religious freedom is the summit of all freedoms," is a central theme in a ninety-three-page document on the Church's future in the Near East, which in recent days Benedict XVI carried into the burning Orient like an Olympic flame. On Friday evening he signed it on Mount Lebanon above Beirut in a circle of many dignitaries. He repeats his watchman's cry for religious freedom often on his journey to this paradisiacal region of crises, where he reminds the President of Lebanon, as a representative for all the governments in the region, that this freedom "is the fundamental freedom on which many others depend." It must be possible for everyone to profess his religion and to live it freely, without putting his life and freedom in danger. "Religious freedom has a societal and political dimension that is indispensable for peace!" It is the freedom even to be able to believe in nothing without being threatened as a result, and the old man defends it here more passionately than almost any atheist has ever done.

He reminds Christendom, however, of something that it has long since almost completely forgotten, given the tumult of the Muslim world. Namely that the oldest Christian community to this day speaks Arabic, the language of the Qur'an. That however offers no protection. No community today is exposed to as many threats and dangers as the Arab Christians, who did not come as missionaries with troops of allied nations into the Orient, but rather were already here before Mohammed fled from Mecca to Medina. The Near East may be the land of Islam's origin. It also remains the cradle of the Jews and of all those united by the belief that God became man two thousand years ago in Jesus of Nazareth.

The awareness has never faded among the many different Churches here that the thread of their origin goes back to Jerusalem. For the oldest set of these Churches, the cultic language of their liturgies is Greek—although their faithful mainly speak and understand Arabic also. In contrast, the majority of Oriental Christians are Catholic and speak and sing in Arabic only. The so-called Latins, as Roman Catholic Christians are called here, are only a small minority among them, although in Europe and the rest of the world they are usually considered the Catholics plain and simple. A remarkable error, as the Pope points out here. For the secret of the Catholics is instead precisely their enormous diversity, especially in many particular Churches "in their own right." Lebanon demonstrates this in an exemplary fashion as no other country does. In this vast mosaic of an overwhelming number of rites and traditions, there are the Copts of Alexandria, the Melkites, Syrians and Maronites of Antioch, the Chaldeans of Babylon, or the Armenians of Cilicia. All of them are Catholics. "Unity does not mean uniformity," the Pope writes in their guest book. Nowhere, therefore, are there as many patriarchs and bishops (and of course as many quarrels) as in Lebanon. All of them use Arabic as a *lingua franca* with one another. There are no strangers in the land. "In this respect the Church in the Near East is exemplary for other local Churches in the rest of the world," the Pope says. In order to strengthen the filigree web of this fascinating societal laboratory, he flew to Beirut at a moment of utmost crisis.

The display of security is overwhelming. The highways are blocked off. Every few meters an armed soldier on the alert, on the rooftops sharpshooters survey the surrounding area. The security officials have seldom had their automatic weapons in firing position so close to the Pope. But as of Saturday, the only shooting was from confetti canons—for instance as the Pope drove past the Presidential Palace in Baabda in his popemobile between columns of cavalrymen. No guest since the visit of John Paul II — toward the end of the civil war, in 1997 — has embodied more hope, which many, many Muslims share with many, many Christians. The a cappella performance of the Gospel of John that was sung in the Melkite Basilica of Saint Paul on the Harissa Hill above Beirut could have sounded to European ears like a surah from the Qur'an. The voices go through your bones to the very marrow. The choirs of Maronites sound as though a belly dance might start any minute. Benedict the Mozart fan listens to them with a shy smile.

Full of compassion he acknowledges the "pangs of a never-ending birth" that the people of the Near East so obviously have been suffering for years and decades. Yet what he also sees in front of him here appears to him like a prophetic model for worldwide Christian ecumenism in general. He therefore evokes the future of the Church in the pluralistic world as an open house of dialogue "with our Jewish and Muslim brethren," among whom "Lebanon more than ever is called to be an example." His fearless courage causes a stir far beyond Beirut, to which he has now brought one of the most mature documents about the Near East. It is a bold and equally realistic roadmap for Christians into an uncertain future. It is the result of countless analyses and experiences that the bishops of the Orient brought to their Synod in Rome two years ago, when he writes laconically: "The attention of the whole world is fixed on the Middle East as it seeks its path. May this region demonstrate that coexistence is not a utopia, and that distrust and prejudice are not a foregone conclusion."

For that, however, he emphasizes many times, a positive strengthening of Christian identity is a prerequisite, even amid the greatest difficulties and sacrifices. Christian faith, he makes clear both to patriarchs and to enthusiastic young people, can never be a mere condition, but rather is always an act as well and an exertion of the will beneath the Cross—amid "cries of pain and desperate faces." There, as he bids them farewell, he encourages the Christians with Jesus' words: "Be not afraid, little flock!"

Babba Jallah (or: revolution of love)—
Beirut, September 16, 2012

Beirut is scarcely recognizable. The glittering metropolis bears almost no resemblance now to the smoking hell from the time of the civil war. High-rise towers gleam in front of the coastal promenade. Bells toll. In the distance a muezzin calls. For the guests from Rome it is as though summer has returned for a few days. The traffic and the honking beneath the window hardly let up all night. Techno music drones from a nearby discotheque. Behind St. George Bay Lebanon looms, up to the last cedar forests on the heights, past which the old state road leads to Damascus. Container ships out at sea glide toward Beirut. In the yacht harbor you can jump from one deck to the next of the elegant boats. In the restaurants the sensual city is on display, as though cosmetics had been invented here. In front of the hotel a bronze statue where Rafiq Hariri was blown up. Other than that there is no splinter, no charred windowsill, nothing left from the attack that once again harrowed Lebanon years ago. Concrete blocks from the old roadblocks still stand here and there beside the street, as though the blockades could be resumed tomorrow. Otherwise: peace. All wars far away, as long as you don't turn on a television.

The Pope will have spared himself that aggravation in recent days, and yet he has no illusions. This is no fairy tale from the *Thousand and One Nights* through which his journey has led like a triumphal procession. He indulges in no dreams, even when he visits the most beautiful hills around Beirut, from Harissa to Baabda to Bkerké, in a veritable marathon of meetings, as though everyone had been waiting for him for years. The local media are head over heels about his "historical" and "glorious" visit in a dangerous time. The fact that he ventured it at all! He keeps waving to the people even when it must seem to him that his arm is falling off. Now and then he raises his eyebrows high as if in greeting, as though in the immense throng he had recognized someone. He smiles; he seems gaunt; at the conclusion he seems rejuvenated by several years. "Babba Jallah!" many placards exclaim to him. This is how many Lebanese would probably cheer on a race horse that they were rooting for. He is protected in every way that one can protect a human being, yet during the concluding Mass on Sunday morning by the sea he presents himself defenseless in front of the thousands of windows in the nearby high-rise apartment buildings on the bay, as though on a serving dish, while in his final homily he recalls "the hour of the Church's birth" on the Cross in nearby Jerusalem and "the suffering Messiah."

"Let us implore the gift of peace for the inhabitants of Syria and the neighboring countries!" he exclaims afterward in his final major prayer in Beirut.

> Sadly, the din of weapons continues to make itself heard, along with the cry of the widow and the orphan. Violence and hatred invade people's lives, and the first victims are women and children. Why so much horror? Why so many

dead? ... Those who wish to build peace must cease to see in the other an evil to be eliminated.... May God grant to your country, to Syria and to the Middle East the gift of peaceful hearts, the silencing of weapons and the cessation of all violence!

To Mary, the Mother of Jesus, the Queen of Heaven and "Cedar of Lebanon" (many Lebanese are convinced that her praises were already sung in the most beautiful melodies by the Jews in the Song of Songs), he consecrates at his departure the sorely tried lands between the coast and the desert and prays "for harmonious coexistence among brothers, whatever their origins and religious convictions." In the days just before he had tirelessly addressed the most important representatives of the country, the President, the Patriarchs, both Christians and Muslims, to recommend to them in one heroic exertion the chief concern of this journey: his passionate defense of freedom of religion for the welfare of every society. Lebanon, however, has provided proof of this under the most difficult conditions longer than any other country of the Orient!

He hands the assembled bishops of the Near East a document in which he, in an era of menacing new trends toward uniformity, prophetically publicizes Lebanon as a model for the diversity of the Orient, from which the whole Church, Europe, and the rest of the world could learn so much. And of course as soon as possible all the close and distant neighbors of the cedar state.

He seemed most relaxed, however, the evening before, when in front of the palace of the Maronites in Bkerké among olive and pine trees he met with the young people, Christians as well as Muslims, Lebanese, Syrians, and Iraqis, in a sea of fluttering white flags, in contrast to and yet reminiscent of the licking flames in the rest of the Orient. Young people as far as the eye can see. In the distance the Mediterranean, and behind that: eternity. The soul of the Near East. The world has not seen a more hopeful image in recent days in any other metropolis of the Eastern world. The Pope's face in the evening sun. "Dear Friends," he exclaimed to the young people time after time. He implored them not to taste the "bitter honey" of emigration and uprooting for the sake of an uncertain future. He exhorted them to fearlessness and a "revolution of love … in the bright, demanding light of the cross." No frustration should mislead them "to flee into alternative universes, to drugs of any sort or into the shabby world of pornography." He warned against the dangers of mistaking virtual reality for the real world. He greeted the Syrian refugees, he greeted the Muslims. "Together with the young Christians, you are the future of this fine country and of the Middle East in general…. It is time for Muslims and Christians to come together so as to put an end to violence and war…. Brotherhood is a foretaste of heaven."

This is his farewell. He did not come as a magician to the cedar state and leaves behind him here no safe and sound world, nor any miracle. Nevertheless, the little man in white provided the land with a fresh supply of hope and self-confidence, as the most necessary resource for the future of Eastern Christians. And with the certainty that the Church is not an agent of any major power on this earth. She is a mourner here.

His steps get ever smaller, but he takes them more and more purposefully and directly, and a cane with a beautiful ivory handle was given to him as a gift. It is moving to see how he gets around with it. For he does not really lean on it; he does not yet know how to do that at all. Instead he carries the cane in front of him. Evidently he still has no idea what it means to walk with a cane.

Benedict Up Close

Jubilee of the Council — Rome, October 11, 2012

A little déjà-vu on a big square, as a Catholic variation on the Jewish ascent to Zion: an endless procession of Synod Bishops, making their pilgrim way up to the altar island in front of Saint Peter's Basilica, in fluttering green robes and white miters, to the hymn with a refrain repeated a hundred times: "*Credo, Domine, adauge nobis fidem.*" (I believe, Lord; increase our faith.) The reddish-purple peacock feathers of the Swiss Guards gleam in the sunlight. It is a radiant October day like the one fifty years ago, an eternal present: the feast of the living God on one "splendid day."

But of course there are no repetitions in Church history. This time the successors of the Apostles Peter and Andrew end the procession: the Pope from Rome and the Ecumenical Patriarch Bartholomew I from Constantinople in his royal vesture from ancient Byzantium. The two men do it in a harmony that still would have been completely unthinkable in 1962 at the beginning of the Council. Even the Anglican Primate Rowan Williams from Canterbury has come to the ceremony. On this morning it is perhaps the most visible fruit of the Second Vatican Council that began here fifty years ago: a new unity of the Roman Church with the Orthodox world, which for almost a thousand years previously seemed unthinkable. The square is not as full as in 1962, but to make up for that the television network EWTN is broadcasting the ceremony at the beginning of this "Year of Faith" to more than two hundred million households worldwide.

Formerly there were more than two thousand Council Fathers; fourteen of the sixty-nine still living have likewise managed to accept once again the invitation to travel to Rome. The remaining fifty-five are by now too weak and frail to make the long journey. But they were all invited to gather by the priest who at that time was the youngest professor at the University of Bonn, whom Cardinal Frings had brought with him to the Council in Rome in 1962 as his consultant: Joseph Ratzinger, whose name today is Benedict XVI. After him there will not be another Pope who helped to shape the Council. Nevertheless, the old gentleman in the shoes of the fisherman cannot get sentimental about that now.

With self-assurance and quiet dignity he has kept his distance for a long time from all those who are of the opinion that they must explain and interpret for him the spirit of the Council. He himself, in contrast, published on the day of this ceremony nearby Saint Peter's Square in a special supplement of *L'Osservatore Romano* a brilliant analysis of the most important spiritual event of the Catholic Church in the twentieth century; because of its sometimes critical tone, it would be hard to find an editor of a German church newspaper willing to reprint what the Pope has to say about the Second Vatican Council, which for many people has long since become a watershed between an old, outmoded Church and the Church afterward. The Pope soberly insists on the identity of the one Church through all time.

In the 1950's, he writes, Christianity "appeared weary and it looked as if the future would be determined by other spiritual forces." The Council's point of departure and real expectation was to be able to bring about once again a decisive turning point in this regard. "The Church, which during the Baroque era was still, in a broad sense, shaping the world, had from the nineteenth century onwards visibly entered into a negative relationship with the modern era, which had only then properly begun. Did it have to remain so? Could the Church not take a positive step into the new era?" Behind the vague expression "today's world" stands however, in his opinion, the question of the Christian relation to the modern era. In order to clarify it, "it would have been necessary to define more clearly the essential features that constitute the modern era." But that is precisely what this Council "did not succeed" in doing. Even though the Council Fathers "expressed many important elements for an understanding of the 'world,'" they "failed to offer substantial clarification on this point."

On the other hand he has a much more positive view of the contribution of Vatican II to religious liberty, which was formulated again here in a completely new and binding way as an essential right among the "fundamental human rights and freedoms." At that time this was as visionary as it was revolutionary: a necessary breakthrough of humanity into the future. This breakthrough, however, lay precisely in the inner nature of the Christian faith, "which had come into being claiming that the State could neither decide on the truth nor prescribe any kind of worship.... Christians prayed for the emperor, but did not worship him. To this extent, it can be said that Christianity, at its birth, brought the principle of religious freedom into the world." He sees critically also that the "precise and extraordinarily dense document" *Nostra aetate* (On the Relation of the Catholic Church to Non-Christian Religions) "speaks of religion solely in a positive way and it disregards the sick and distorted forms of religion which, from the historical and theological viewpoints, are of far-reaching importance."

Farewell and Ascent on the
Mountain of Prayer — 2013

Resignation — Rome, February 11, 2013

A tremendous thunderclap shook the black winter sky over the papal palace that evening. A gigantic lightning bolt struck the top of the dome of Saint Peter's. It was pouring buckets. Rome was in shock. When John Paul II died, the Eternal City broke out into spontaneous applause on densely crowded Saint Peter's Square. Now mourning falls over the people. A sorrow that does not know what comes next. Perplexity. Nothing had prepared Rome for it, or the 1.2 billion Catholics on all continents. "Like lightning from a clear sky" the news about the resignation of Benedict XVI surprised even the cardinals in the Baroque Sala del Consistorio in the papal palace, said Cardinal Sodano in his first reaction to the announcement. Because Benedict XVI toward the end of a meeting read aloud the personal letter in Latin, softly, in his weak voice, quite a few cardinals probably also wondered whether they had understood correctly what they had just heard. The Pope is resigning! Impossible! How is that supposed to happen? With Benedict XVI a lot happened that "doesn't happen"; from the very start you could rely on him for surprises.

Until then the meeting had proceeded in a venerable, "business-as-usual" fashion. Cardinal Amato had introduced to the assembled cardinals the future new saints of the Catholic Church: the eight hundred martyrs from Otranto in Southern Italy who in 1480 preferred to be beheaded by Muslim invaders than to renounce their Catholic faith. Many were already looking at the clock. One or another of them probably thought of his next conversation partner, with whom he had an appointment for lunch. But with his last dramatic step, Benedict XVI crossed out one last time the plans of all the Vatican analysts and of his countless enemies and friends worldwide. In a way he resigned from his position just as he had been assigned to it.

When he was elected, many of the wisest heads in the world tried to figure out what "career plan" had enabled the clever little man from Germany with the snow-white hair and the gentle eyes to catapult himself into the highest position of the Universal Church. The truth was: he did not have one. That alone made him one-of-a-kind in the Vatican. Today he is likewise unique in his unprecedented willingness to hand over his authority to a stronger successor. He was serious when he made the announcement, but no weaker than on other days, and no more infirm. On Saturday he had still greeted 4,500 Knights of Malta in Saint Peter's Basilica and that evening had given extemporaneously to the major seminarians of Rome a little summary of his theology, at the highest height of his intellectual power. On Sunday as usual he had prayed with the faithful on Saint Peter's Square the Angelus at his window, and before that had explained the Gospel reading for the day, which tells us that "failures and difficulties must not lead us to discouragement.... Our job is to cast the nets in faith. The Lord does the rest." He saw that the time had now come. He did, he must be thinking, what he had to do. His initiatives are countless. He lowered one net after another from the Barque of Peter into the depths of the global sea. The harvest no longer belongs to him. Other personnel must now bring in those nets.

He always did everything carefully, but never a step like this one. He chose February 11 as the day for the announcement of his resignation. That is the Memorial of Our Lady of Lourdes, who for well over a hundred years has become the ardent desire of countless sick and infirm people. Now, in solidarity, Benedict XVI includes himself among these infirm persons with his landmark decision — in full possession of his mental faculties, but physically too weak for the superhumanly important tasks of a pope. It is obvious that he reflected on and weighed his plan maturely. It seems now in retrospect almost as if he were resigning according to a carefully prepared script — which however he himself wrote. "If a Pope clearly realizes that he is no longer physically, psychologically, and spiritually capable of handling the duties of his office," he said to Peter Seewald in the summer of 2010 in Castel Gandolfo, "then he has a right and, under some circumstances, also an obligation to resign." He now saw himself so obliged.

Mentally and intellectually he is perfectly alert and oriented — everyone who still comes near him confirms this — but it has also become increasingly evident to everyone, even from a distance, that he has been losing his physical strength more and more. And obviously he regards the state of the Church, which faces major challenges, as too critical for him to consider it wise, after his eight-year pontificate, to be at the head of the Church in his condition, in a deteriorating agony, as his predecessor John

Paul II so distressingly did before him. For he knows this too: His way of the cross may possibly last several more years—even though he has already refused to take life-prolonging daily medications, for instance to treat his heart flutter.

The challenges made on the Pope, however, change in intensity almost daily. Therefore it seemed to his brother Georg in Regensburg from the start as though the new job of being the successor of Peter would completely overtax his smart little brother for the first time. Other than in prayer, Benedict XVI has discussed the matter only with his brother. The latter listened to him and advised him neither for nor against, but ultimately the decision did not surprise him. It had already been made "several months ago." That dismisses immediately all the speculations claiming that the very serious breaches of trust from the inner sanctum of the Church which the Pope had to cope with over the course of the Vatileaks scandal might possibly have driven him to resign. The damage done was terrible. But he is resigning because his strength is failing, not because he was deceived and disappointed. And not in order to escape martyrdom. Nor is he retiring sulkily, but rather in an unprecedentedly reasonable, cool and deliberate act of sovereignty, without regard to the judgments of others—in an extremely modern step.

In this sense he is not resigning, either, but rather freely going ahead into the inner sanctum of the Church's prayer. It is incomprehensible and unprecedented, but I don't care. It is just sad. It sticks like a lump in the throat. The Poles together with their Pope brought about the collapse of the Soviet Union. Instead of that, the Germans have recently taken an increasingly hostile attitude toward Benedict XVI, the Catholics almost even more than the Protestants. It is enough to make you weep. Yet triumphs were not his thing. Benedict was not able to reconcile Germany with himself. Instead he succeeded at something much softer that will move Christendom even more in the future. In his short reign Benedict brought talk about "the Face of God" back into the world, since September 1, 2006, the day when he, as the first pope in over four hundred years, bent his knee before the rediscovered veil of Veronica, the old crown jewel of the popes. Since then he has not stopped talking about it. In his next-to-last audience he mentioned it twenty-five times! With the Face of God in the Face of Jesus of Nazareth he has made widely available again the unique selling point of Christianity. It has — truly — become the seal of his pontificate.

Ash Wednesday — Rome, February 13, 2013

The hair of Benedict XVI is so brilliantly white that the ashes that Cardinal Comastri strewed on his head before the main altar in Saint Peter's Basilica can be perceived only as a tiny shadow. He looks into my eyes. The golden paten that a deacon holds between us reflects the play of light from the dome back onto his features. He is centuries old. His eyes remind me of the eyes of my mother. "*Corpus Christi*," he says as I kneel down. "Amen," I respond; then he, with unwavering gaze, places the host from the ciborium onto my tongue. I cannot take my eyes off him. He looks at me until I turn away.

It is his last Mass over the tomb of the Apostle Peter. He will return only once more — to this very spot where he now distributes Holy Communion to the faithful one last time. That will be when he pauses once more, like his predecessors, on his way to his final rest somewhere here in Saint Peter's Basilica, while the faithful make their pilgrim way past his bier. Anyone who could, came already today. "Remember, man, that you are dust, and unto dust you shall return," is the greeting whispered to the faithful of the Catholic Church when the cross of ashes is traced on their forehead. Or: "Repent and believe in the Gospel." Benedict XVI personally embodies and unites the two sentences this Wednesday. He is Peter, the Rock — one last time. Yet today he has already become utterly and entirely a living sign: the Gospel made flesh.

That is why the ceremony at the Basilica of Santa Sabina — where according to an age-old Roman custom it is celebrated every year on Ash Wednesday by the Successor of Peter — had to be transferred to the largest basilica in Christendom, over the tomb of Peter himself, because this time many thousands of people wanted to see and experience him during this final act of distributing ashes. Beneath the wintry sun a never-ending line formed on Saint Peter's Square as people tried to press their way into the Basilica once more for the farewell of Benedict XVI. With the ashes of burned olive branches from the hills along the Via Appia, Rome begins the liturgical cycle that leads to the feast of the Resurrection of Christ from the dead on Easter Sunday. Today Pope Benedict leads this pilgrimage one last time for the Catholic Church. Centuries-old Gregorian chants accompany him. His familiar voice, fragile with age, is firmer and stronger than it has been in a long time, even in the longer passages that the eighty-five-year-old still had to sing by himself.

The Latin litany invokes a selection from the enormous crowd of witnesses — from Abraham through the desert fathers Saba and Antony down to Saint Elizabeth — who have gone before today's pilgrims into the Heavenly Jerusalem. One last time the Pope climbs the steps of the altar in front of them, vested in the violet penitential garments of the Lenten season, his eyes downcast, his hand firmly on his shepherd's staff, and incenses the sacrificial table beneath the Bernini heaven. Countless bishops and cardinals accompanied him in this procession. He is impressively handsome [*schön*]; there is scarcely any other way to put it. Unearthly seriousness fills Saint Peter's Basilica. The announcement of his resignation lends tension to the liturgy, an unprecedented intensification of the awareness of the last time—the last time!

Suddenly for everyone present it is a never-before-seen cosmic drama presided over by Benedict XVI this evening "on a path of repentance," as he says in one of his prayers. He stands erect like a Swiss Guard, listens while seated with intense concentration to the readings from Scripture, his hands flat on his knees ("Behold, now is the day of salvation!"); he gives thanks in his last homily and once more begs for the prayers of the faithful for the Church's path and unity. It is a sparkling prism beneath the dome of Saint Peter's, in which he lets his theology shine once more in farewell, warns against "religious hypocrisy" and from Rome exhorts the Universal Church together with the prophet: "Rend your hearts, not your garments!" Hundreds of times in recent years he has extolled "the Face of God." Now, though, he exhorts his listeners to make the "countenance of the Church," too, which has been disfigured by tensions, rivalries, and divisions, shine once again before the world. May it be a witness, which will "always be more effective, the less we seek our own glory." Now is the time for this. "Behold, now is a very acceptable time; behold, now is the day of salvation."

After him the Cardinal Secretary of State Tarcisio Bertone offers a short word of thanks in a tone never before heard at the Pope's side, as he exclaims to him with tears in his voice:

"Were we not to tell you, Your Holiness, that this evening our hearts are veiled in sorrow, we would not be sincere.... Thank you for giving us the shining example of a simple and humble worker in the Lord's vineyard, a worker, however, who was able at every moment to do what is most important: to bring God to men and women and to bring men and women to God.... Your Magisterium has been a window open on the Church and on the world; it has let the rays of truth and of God's love stream in, giving light and warmth to us as we go on our way, even and especially when clouds are gathering above." Love and devotion were also what prompted him to take his final, most difficult step.

It is as though the verbal power of the departing Pope had flashed over to him as he extolled his courage and humility, "which have distinguished every step of your life and your ministry. They cannot but come from closeness to God, from living in the light of the word of God, from constantly ascending the mountain of the encounter with him, to come down later to the city of men." Utterly unliturgical applause then breaks out on Ash Wednesday in Saint Peter's Basilica—which after the blessing continues to surge in a never-ending ebb and flow, for minutes, for hours, an eternity. Tears everywhere you look. Archbishop Müller fights back tears just like Archbishop Gänswein. A wave of affection breaks over the old, shyly smiling Pontiff after his last greeting of peace as he slowly glides down the middle of Saint Peter's Basilica toward the exit, blessing the crowd, and disappears. Outside, on Saint Peter's Square, in six weeks, on Palm Sunday, Jesus' entrance into Jerusalem will be commemorated with fresh branches from the olive trees along the Via Appia. But by the next Pope then and the next Successor of Peter and of Benedict XVI.

Troppo puro, troppo innocente, troppo santo —
Rome, February 23, 2013

The 348th General Audience of Benedict XVI is his last, and nothing is as it always was. More than five million people have encountered him in the past eight years in these audiences on Saint Peter's Square or in Nervi Hall. Yet today it seems as though another perceived extra million had arrived to bid him farewell shoulder to shoulder at his last appearance. Only at his burial will he appear once again in public in a similar way, but then of course dead and on the shoulders of the servants of the Papal Household, who will carry his bier down the Scala Regia to the Square, with his mourning followers behind him. Right now death is far away.

The Piazza is throbbing with life. The throngs at the barriers are incredible. It is blazing hot. A forest of flags from all continents waves fluttering over the crowd. The Universal Church bids the Pope farewell — although he has not died. A helicopter circles high up in the cloudless sky. Sea gulls sailing far inland cast their shadows along the marble façade of Saint Peter's Basilica. It is a folk festival of faith: a brilliant first Spring day in this Roman February. And it does not take much imagination to hear the echo of Cardinal Ratzinger, who exclaimed here on April 8, 2005, during the burial of his predecessor: "Now John Paul stands at the window in the Father's house and sees us and blesses us." It cannot be otherwise. His predecessor is probably still watching now and blesses this hour.

Eleven days later — on April 19, 2005 — Joseph Ratzinger then became Pope himself, and another five days later he exclaimed here on this Square at his coronation Mass: "Yes, the Church lives — this is the marvelous experience of these days.

The Church is alive. And She is young. She carries the future of the world within Herself and shows every individual the way to the future!" Now, at his end, he spontaneously and emotionally takes up the cry again when he sees below him the crowd that wants to take leave of him here: "Look at how alive the Church is!" Rome is full, as it was at the canonization of Padre Pio. The people cram the broad Via della Conciliazione down to the Tiber, as panorama shots by cameras at high vantage points show on the jumbo-screens that enlarge the now-cheerful face of the little old Pope. Italy especially bows here today one last time to the man who now has become definitively for many a "*Papa angelicus*" [Latin: "angelic Pope"]. He is a "*Papa d'amore*" [Italian: "Pope of love"], an old fisherman from Ladispoli to my left insists, and to my right tears welled up earlier in the eyes of a gray-haired police chief as the stooped old man in white, standing in his popemobile, drove through the cordoned-off streets into the crowd, his left hand firmly on the railing, his right hand raised in blessing. He is "*troppo puro, troppo innocente, troppo santo!*" ("too pure, too innocent, too holy"), the man exclaimed and wiped his eyes, as the crowd around us jumped as one man onto the chairs in the front part of the Square, men and women, elderly and children, priests and laypeople, believers from all continents. Jubilation interrupts the Pope again and again later on, too. "Through this Pope I learned to love the Germans," said one young Italian woman.

The drive to his armchair in front of the main entrance to the Basilica lasted almost an hour, before he saluted the crowd in his gravelly voice with a Latin greeting of peace, as always. His mind broadened on this day to embrace the Church throughout the world. First, though, he listened again even today to a reading from the Letter of the Apostle Paul to the Colossians, and then he explained the Scriptures for a last time and once again introduced Peter, his predecessor from the Sea of Gennesaret in Galilee. He too already knew that the boat that he steered belonged not to him but to the Lord. So it is in general with the Church: It does not belong to the Pope or to the people; it belongs to God alone. "The Church is His boat!"

It is a high point of his decades-long interpretation of Scripture. But today he concludes with a hymn of thanks, to God, to his collaborators, to the cardinals, to the ambassadors who represent the world's population here, and finally to the whole Church, whose "strength is the word of truth in the Gospels." He also thanks them all once again for their respect for his difficult decision and assures them that, although he completely gave up his private life eight years ago for his final ministry as Successor of Peter, he is of course not returning today to his private life, but intends only to pray from now on for the Church. He greets the people one last time in many languages, in Arabic, in Polish (that he learned in his old age especially for the people of his predecessor), and thanks the wind band from Traunstein for their Bavarian anthem. "It is so beautiful to be a Christian!" Then he stands up and intones the Our Father in Latin. A little white man with folded hands and a trembling voice, upright. This image will last.

Humility and charm—Rome, February 28, 2013, 6:00 p.m.

The resignation of Pope Benedict XVI from office is a unique event, but it is not entirely without precedent. He is not retiring in failure, but in complete command like Charles V, who was not a pope but the Emperor—one of the greatest leaders of the West—when he took off his crown on October 25, 1555, to withdraw to a monastery in Spain.

It was one of the most stirring scenes in the history of Europe. In 1530 Charles V had been crowned the last Roman-German Emperor by the Pope. His empire, on which the sun never set, extended over several continents. During his reign the division of Christendom in Europe came about. The conquest of Mexico and of the Incan Empire, the "*Sacco di Roma*" [Sack of Rome] and the defeat of the Turks also occurred during his regency. Now, in his court in Brussels, bent over with gout, wearing black velvet, in mourning as though for his own burial and leaning on William of Orange, he handed over imperial rule to his son Philip. His retrospect at his farewell must therefore be quoted here briefly verbatim.

> Forty years ago I became King of Spain, then Emperor—not to govern even more kingdoms, but to look after the welfare of Germany and of the other kingdoms, to maintain and create the peace and concord of all Christendom and to turn its forces against the Turks. I had great hopes. Only a few of them have been fulfilled, and I have only a few left. This finally made me weary and sick. I have borne with all disorders as much as humanly possible until today, so that no one could say that I was a deserter. But now it would be irresponsible to delay my abdication even longer. My strength is simply no longer adequate. I know that I have made many blunders, great blunders, first on account of my youth, then due to human error and because of my passions, and finally out of weariness. But I have deliberately done no one an injustice, whoever it may be. If nevertheless injustice has come about, it happened without my knowledge and only out of ineptitude: I publicly regret it and ask everyone whom I may have offended for his forgiveness.

Charles V did not actually become a monk after that, but he did retire to the monastery of San Jerónimo de Yuste in a remote corner of Spain, where from his bed he immersed himself for the last three years of his life in the eyes of the reviled head of Christ, streaming with blood, in the countenance of the tormented King of Kings, before whom on September 21, 1558, the once most powerful leader in Europe finally closed his eyes forever. *Ecce homo!* [Behold the man!]

The parallels were conspicuous when Benedict XVI appeared two weeks earlier in his fur-lined red mozetta and festive papal surplice in his palace in the presence of the cardinals. He was the first pope of the new millennium. The sun never set on his "kingdom" either, which was nevertheless not entirely of this world. The Roman Catholic Church had never been larger. New and unprecedented challenges had awaited the Pontifex Maximus. He was a principal bridge-builder between worlds that were drifting apart, which Benedict XVI had clearly in view when he read aloud in Latin the following declaration:

> After having repeatedly examined my conscience before God, I have come to the certainty that my strengths, due to an advanced age, are no longer suited to an adequate exercise of the Petrine ministry. I am well aware that this ministry, due to its essential spiritual nature, must be carried out not only with words and deeds, but no less with prayer and suffering. However, in today's world, subject to so many rapid changes and shaken by questions of deep relevance for the life of faith, in order to govern the Barque of Saint Peter and proclaim the Gospel, both strength of mind and body are necessary, strength which in the last few months has deteriorated in me to

the extent that I have had to recognize my incapacity to adequately fulfill the ministry entrusted to me. For this reason, and well aware of the seriousness of this act, with full freedom I declare that I renounce the ministry of Bishop of Rome, Successor of Saint Peter, entrusted to me by the Cardinals on 19 April 2005.... I thank you most sincerely for all the love and work with which you have supported me in my ministry and I ask pardon for all my defects.

Now he would set out for the mountain of prayer to which he feels called by God.

His biography seems to have unfolded under an overarching cosmos of signs. Even the weather played along, from the rainbow over Auschwitz when he spoke up in Birkenau as the Pope from Germany, to the lightning that struck the dome of Saint Peter's on the evening of his resignation. He was born on a Holy Saturday, between Good Friday and Easter. It was April 16 but also the feast day of little Bernadette Soubirous, the visionary of Lourdes. The feast of Our Lady of Lourdes, though, is February 11, the day on which Benedict XVI announced his resignation. On February 28, 1982, he had taken leave in Munich as Archbishop of Munich and Freising; thirty-one years later he now took leave in the Vatican on February 28, 2013, as Bishop of Rome and Pope of the Universal Church. The timing of a celestial stage director seems to rule his life, in which the great conservative nevertheless viewed his final office in a more sober and modern way than many of his predecessors.

He may never have doubted that as successor of the Apostle Peter he embodied the rock on which Jesus of Nazareth founded His Church, according to the Catholic understanding. As a theologian, though, he knew also how weak Peter was. According to the testimony of the Gospels he was the only human being for whom Jesus Himself prayed. But a rock is a rock. When Benedict XVI realized that he was crumbling, he logically retired, given the many challenges, so as to clear the way for a rock-solid successor. He is not fleeing his office; he enriched it. Rome is in flames, but he is not abandoning it; he does not need to hear Jesus ask him at the city limits, "Where are you going?" ("*Quo vadis?*"), but rather he is moving to the inner sanctum of the Church to pray. "And you, strengthen your brethren," was Jesus' last command to Peter. Benedict is now obeying this command in prayer. His witness (*martyrium*) is consequently not yet at an end. But he steps back from the window of the papal palace too, so as not to compete up there in the years to come with the heroic agony of his predecessor. This humility took courage. And grace.

His legacy? "*Aufklärung*" [Enlightenment, clarification] is the German word that perhaps plays the biggest role in it, as in the life of Joseph Ratzinger. The concept was also like a guiding star above his pontificate. A radical enlightenment of the Catholic Church about itself is the lasting heritage in the work of the slight man, in his various offices. Clarification about its own sins, about all forms of abuse, about the byways and dead ends of theology, about the Second Vatican Council, the correct understanding of Tradition, about Christianity's roots in Judaism, about accepting the challenge of a dialogue of Christendom with the House of Islam, which is necessary for survival, an enlightenment about the divine liturgy and about the mystery of evil. At the conclusion he took leave with a bombshell of clarification. He leaves behind for his successor a dossier compiled by three cardinals about the state of the Curia—the sort that he himself could have used when he entered upon his office. Never before had it been as transparent in the Vatican as during his pontificate — and this is true also about the Catholic Church worldwide.

Not everyone liked that, many Germans least of all. Bernd Ulrich wrote about "liberation in Rome" after Benedict XVI gave up his arduous office. Any reader of that front-page article could learn from it also about an unburdening — that was experienced not by the Pope but by the Germans as a result of this step. In fact with this resignation a cultural challenge falls away from the land of the Reformation, a challenge that many Christians — from both denominations — do not feel up to. When Benedict XVI was elected on April 19, 2005, to many observers it seemed as though it finally put an end to the last World War that Germany had begun against the whole world in the last century. At the end of his pontificate it is evident that the war-torn land is still at war with itself. Joseph Ratzinger enlightened us about that too. Many did not go along with this process [of coping with the past]. The nation was not proud of its greatest son in this century. Now the German hour of the Universal Church is over. As far as his former homeland is concerned, Benedict's farewell is reminiscent of the doorkeeper in Kafka's *The Trial*, who at the end of the novel closes the gate with the words: "No one else could gain admission here; this entrance was destined for you alone."

Light from light — Rome, July 5, 2013

The oldest Christian tradition in Jerusalem is a liturgy of light, in which the Church of the Sepulchre is transformed anew each year on Holy Saturday into a volcano. The event is — after the descent of the holy fire into Christ's burial chamber — an explosion of light over tens of thousands of candles in a way that is hardly imaginable in the Christian world of the West. The paschal jubilation of this hour here is almost unimaginable too. On Holy Saturday in 1927, however, Joseph Ratzinger was born also, who after his Encyclicals on love and hope now submits under the title "Light of Faith" (*Lumen Fidei*) a final magisterial document about faith, which his successor Pope Francis enlarged with a few chapters, undersigned and presented as his first Encyclical. It is a premiere marked by rare humility and collaboration.

Nevertheless, the ninety-page document is still the legacy of Benedict XVI, in which the whole theology of the retired pope shines forth. It is his testament, which creeps and climbs like tendrils around light as a central concept of Christendom, whose faith from the very beginning always has been a religion of light. "You are the light of the world," Jesus said to those who followed Him. The Gospels are full of this radiance. "God from God, light from light," it says in the first common profession of the Christian faith in the year 325 about the "Son of God," the "Sun of righteousness." This slim volume therefore mentions this light more than 120 times.

"The pagan world, which hungered for light, had seen the growth of the cult of the sun god, *Sol Invictus*," it says for instance in the introduction to the Encyclical, "invoked each day at sunrise." Yet even though the sun to all appearances was reborn each day, people then still must have understood very well that it was not capable of radiating its light over all of human existence. Indeed, the sun does not illuminate reality as a whole. Its rays, for example, cannot penetrate into the shadow of death, where the human eye is closed to its light. "No one has ever been ready to die for his faith in the sun," Justin Martyr therefore also wrote. The faith, however, for which from the very beginning many were willing to give their lives has become once again in the latest Encyclical of the Catholic Church "arranged for four hands" the comprehensive theme of the old piano player in a final great composition that his successor now addresses to all bishops, priests, deacons, nuns, hermits "and all believers in Christ" throughout the world.

It is the faith in which "the risen Christ" is "the morning star" of humanity, which illuminates every aspect of human existence down into death itself, because "the history of Jesus is the complete manifestation of God's reliability." It is a faith that looks at the world with the eyes of Jesus, in "a participation in his way of seeing." In many areas of life we trust others, the document says, "who know more than we do." We trust the architect who builds our house, the pharmacist who provides healing medicine, the lawyer who defends us in court. "We also need someone trustworthy and knowledgeable where God is concerned. Jesus, the Son of God, is the one who makes God known to us [*der uns Gott 'erklärt'*]."

This is the unmistakable tone of Joseph Ratzinger who speaks here once again to us, juggling for us as confidently as a circus performer with quotations from Nietzsche, Dante, Rousseau, Dostoyevsky, John Henry Newman, Romano Guardini, or T. S. Eliot, only to remark in passing briefly and succinctly: "Once I think that by turning away from God I will find myself, my life begins to fall apart." Or: "The self-awareness of the believer now expands because of the presence of another; it now lives in this other and thus, in love, life takes on a whole new breadth.... For those who have been transformed in this way, a new way of seeing opens up, faith becomes light for their eyes." Or: "Today more than ever, we need to be reminded of this bond between faith and truth, given the crisis of truth in our age." Once again it is a necklace of pearls in that familiar language of Ratzinger, which his life as Pope did not make any easier for him, before he announced on

February 11 his resignation from this superhumanly difficult post along with his ascent to the "mountain of prayer."

On December 25, 2005, when he signed his first Encyclical on love, he recalled Dante's *Divine Comedy*, in which the pilgrim encounters in the middle of the light of paradise a face, whereupon the then almost eighty-year-old Pope exclaimed with astonishment like a child: "God, the infinite light, possesses a human face." In his last Encyclical on faith, he evokes this "human Face of God" again, sixteen times, and says: "The light of faith is the light of a countenance in which the Father is seen." It is "the light of a word, because it is the light of a personal countenance, a light which, even as it enlightens us, calls us and seeks to be reflected on our faces and to shine from within us." This formulation, however, in the legacy of the old Joseph "Benedict" Ratzinger, is almost pure Dante Alighieri, who in the early fourteenth century describes in Canto XXXIII of his *Paradiso* the countenance that met him within the divine light: "Within itself, and in its own color, / Seemed to be painted with our effigy [i.e., likeness]; / And so absorbed my attention altogether." (*Dentro da se del suo colore istesso / Mi parve pinta della nostra effige / Per che il mio viso in lei tutto era messo.*)

It is the same light that on the "Sabbath of Light" in Jerusalem is passed from flame to flame. So too it is with the faith, the new Encyclical says. " 'Faith is passed on ... by contact, from one person to another, just as one candle is lighted from another." It is the light without which we all would not exist, in which the universe is distinguished from nothingness. And it is a last genial idea [*Einfall*] of Joseph Ratzinger to entitle his last Encyclical in this way, because light itself was the first and last incursion [*Einfall*] of God into this world, one that reaches down into the realm of death.

AUG -- 2017